SIMPLY PHO

A COMPLETE COURSE IN PREPARING
AUTHENTIC VIETNAMESE MEALS AT HOME

HELEN LE

Race Point
PUBLISHING

Brimming with creative inspiration, how-to projects, and useful information to enrich your everyday life, Quarto Knows is a favorite destination for those pursuing their interests and passions. Visit our site and dig deeper with our books into your area of interest: Quarto Creates, Quarto Cooks, Quarto Homes, Quarto Lives, Quarto Drives, Quarto Explores, Quarto Gifts, or Quarto Kids.

© 2017 by Helen Le

First published in 2017 by Race Point Publishing, an imprint of The Quarto Group, 142 West 36th Street, 4th Floor, New York, NY 10018, USA
T (212) 779-4972 **F** (212) 779-6058 **www.QuartoKnows.com**

10 9 8 7 6 5 4

ISBN: 978-1-63106-370-1

Library of Congress Cataloging-in-Publication Data

Names: Le, Helen, 1984- author.
Title: Simply pho : a complete course in preparing authentic Vietnamese meals
   at home / Helen Le.
Description: New York : Race Point Publishing, 2017. | Includes index.
Identifiers: LCCN 2017015604 | ISBN 9781631063701 (hardback)
Subjects: LCSH: Cooking, Vietnamese. | Noodle soups--Vietnam. | BISAC:
   COOKING / Regional & Ethnic / Vietnamese. | COOKING / Regional & Ethnic /
   Asian. | COOKING / Courses & Dishes / Soups & Stews. | LCGFT: Cookbooks.
Classification: LCC TX724.5.V5 L425 2017 | DDC 641.59597--dc23
LC record available at https://lccn.loc.gov/2017015604

Editorial Director: Jeannine Dillon
Creative Director: Merideth Harte
Project Editor: Erin Canning
Food Photographer: Evi Abeler, Big Leo Productions
Food Stylist: Julia Choi
Assistant Food Stylist: Erika Joyce
Food Stylist Interns: Sami Ginsberg and Alyssa Kondracki
Vietnam Photographer: Ha Tien Anh
Cover Design: Merideth Harte
Interior Design: Roger Walton Studio
Props supplied by Esther Harte and Edward Gallagher

Printed in China

For my mom, who is also my first teacher, faithful kitchen helper, on-occasion video production crew, serious food critic, best friend—my everything.

CONTENTS

INTRODUCTION

I was born and grew up in Da Nang, Vietnam, a coastal city in central Vietnam. I ate pho no more than twice a month since it was just one option among so many food choices there. Besides steamed rice (*cơm*) as a staple food for our everyday meals, we have hundreds of other dishes made from "God's gems" (a sacred name once used for rice). Foods made from rice include thin rice vermicelli (*bún*), steamed rice sheets (*bánh cuốn*), steamed rice cakes with toppings (*bánh bèo*), savory rice crêpes (*bánh xèo*), rice dumplings (*bánh giò*), and so much more.

When I traveled outside of Vietnam for the first time in 2003, for school, and made many friends from around the world, I was surprised that most of them only knew Vietnamese food as pho and fresh spring rolls (*gỏi cuốn*)! I barely even knew what *gỏi cuốn* were before I traveled abroad! In central Vietnam, we eat fresh spring rolls with pork accompanied by anchovy sauce (*bánh tráng cuốn thịt heo*). Most of the people who migrated to Australia and the United States after the Vietnam War were from the South and it's their regional specialties that are so popular in the rest of the world.

The fact is, Vietnamese food differs a lot from region to region and every small town has its own delicacies, which is what makes the cuisine so special. The recipes in this cookbook not only include Western favorites such as pho, spring rolls, and sandwiches, but also lots of soups and dishes made with a variety of noodles, as well as coffee drinks, sweets, and condiments—in other words, a large and delicious sampling of Vietnamese cuisine. And as I continue to grow my YouTube channel, Helen's Recipes, I want to introduce even more amazing dishes to my fans.

Let's begin!

HOW TO MAKE A PERFECT BOWL OF PHO

There's a lot that goes into making a bowl of pho—technique and time—to achieve a clear, flavorful broth with that oh so tantalizing aroma. Here are the tools, techniques, and tips that will help you on your quest for the perfect bowl of soup.

KITCHEN TOOLS

Making pho at home doesn't really require any special equipment. Here are the tools that are essential for a successful bowl of soup.

Stockpot: An 8- to 10-quart (7.5 to 9.5 L) stockpot is a must for cooking pho at home.

Spice filter: When you add the pho aroma ingredients to the broth, you need a container to hold them so that they're easy to remove. Spice filters come in various forms such as re-usable metal spice balls or cloth spice bags. You can also use cheesecloth or large disposable tea or spice bags.

Long-handle noodle strainer: It's always nice to blanch the noodles and warm up the serving bowl before pouring in the hot soup. That's why a noodle strainer comes in handy. Just add the noodles to the strainer and submerge in a pot of boiling water. When you lift up the strainer, let the hot water drip into the empty bowl. Give the bowl a swirl and pour out the hot water. The noodles and bowl are then warmed up, ready for the hot soup.

HOW TO MAKE A CLEAR, FRAGRANT, AND FLAVORFUL BROTH

Besides flavor and aroma, clarity is treasured most in a good broth. Here are the steps to help you achieve a clear, fragrant, and flavorful broth for the perfect bowl of soup.

1. For a traditional beef broth, use a mix of bones (knuckle, marrow, ribs, oxtail, and femur) for a more flavorful broth—the more the merrier. See the Beef Bone Directory on page 14. Of course, you can also make chicken, pork, and fish broths, using the appropriate bones. Choose mature bones with less fat as they give a deeper and sweeter flavor. Soak beef and pork bones in salted water and rinse a few times to cut down on the blood in the bones.

2. Parboil the bones for 5 to 10 minutes. After parboiling them, dump out all the water and rinse the bones well. Many cooks are afraid of losing the flavor with this step, but it is the other way around. During the first 5 to 10 minutes of boiling, the bones release all their impurities and residues. Parboiling helps to cut down on skimming. The bones' true essence only comes out after several hours of cooking.

3. Place the rinsed parboiled bones in a clean stockpot and fill with enough cold water to cover them. Bring to a boil.

4. While bringing to a boil, add a whole peeled onion to enhance the sweetness and keep the broth clear. Add salt and rock sugar (essentially crystallized cane sugar) for flavor. Rock sugar has a milder taste than regular sugar. You can substitute rock sugar with caster (superfine) sugar or brown sugar.

continued on page 15

CLOUDY BROTH

CLEAR BROTH

BEEF BONE DIRECTORY

FEMUR

MARROW

KNUCKLE

OXTAIL

COOKING TIP

If after all this, your broth turns out cloudy, you can fix it by letting it cool and adding egg white (1 egg white per 3 quarts, or 3 L, of broth). Stir and bring to a boil again, then skim or strain, if necessary.

5. When the water comes to a boil, reduce the heat and simmer, uncovered, over low heat, occasionally skimming off the scum. Cooking the broth over high heat will make it cloudy and sour-tasting; cooking the broth uncovered is crucial for a clear broth. The broth will evaporate and reduce in the process of cooking. Make up the difference by adding hot water to the stockpot. (Adding cold water might make the broth cloudy and sour-tasting due to temperature shock.)

6. To get the most out of the bones, here are recommended cooking times: fish bones, 30 minutes; chicken bones, 2 to 3 hours; pork bones, 4 to 5 hours; and beef bones, 8 to 10 hours. However, at home, I only have time to cook pork and beef bones for 1 to 2 hours, which is still acceptable.

7. Char/toast the pho aroma ingredients (roots such as onion and ginger; spices such as cinnamon, star anise, and black cardamom) before adding to the broth for more fragrance. See Pho Aroma: How to Char Roots and Toast Spices on page 16. Optional: Grill dried seafood (such as shrimp, mussels, squid, and sea worm) to remove the fishy smell before adding to the broth for more fragrance and natural sweetness.

8. Add the charred/toasted/grilled items (dried roots, spices, and seafood) at a later stage of simmering the broth, 30 to 45 minutes before finishing (after skimming off all foam).

9. Except for salt and rock sugar, add other seasonings such as chicken stock powder when the broth is done cooking. Fish sauce could cause a sour aftertaste if added too soon, so it's preferable served as a condiment to let diners add it to suit their tastes.

PHO AROMA: HOW TO CHAR ROOTS AND TOAST SPICES

This is an absolute must to get the pho broth's distinctive aroma. In Vietnam, we char the roots directly over an open flame on the stove, and the neighbors can tell what's cooking from the lovely smell. If you have an electric stove, lay a piece of aluminum foil on top of the burner and place the roots on top to char. Another option is to broil them in the oven at 425°F (220°C) for 10 minutes.

As quite a few spices are crucial to achieve the pho aroma, here's a guide to help you remember the basics: For ten servings, you'll need one onion, two thumb-size pieces of ginger (cut lengthwise into ⅛-inch-thick, or 3 mm, slices), three star anise, two cinnamon sticks, and two black cardamom pods. Apart from these, you can experiment with other spices, such as cloves, coriander seeds, and fennel seeds, to see which ones best suit your taste. I consider these spices optional.

1. Heat the onion and ginger slices directly over an open flame on the stove until slightly charred on all sides.

2. Peel the grilled onion, but try to keep the stem intact and not let the onion layers fall apart. Rinse the onion and ginger under warm running water and scrape off the charred bits.

3. Toast the star anise, cinnamon sticks, and black cardamom pods in a large pan over medium-low heat until fragrant, about 2 minutes.

4. Place these spices in a spice ball or large tea or spice bag(s), or wrap in a piece of cheesecloth. Add the spices and the charred onion and ginger to the stockpot 30 to 45 minutes before serving, so the aroma stays fresh and tempting.

2 THUMB-SIZE PIECES OF SLICED GINGER

2 CINNAMON STICKS

2 BLACK CARDAMON PODS

3 STAR ANISE

1 ONION

HOW TO MAKE FRESH PHO NOODLES

SKILL LEVEL: Intermediate • **PREP TIME:** 10 minutes
COOK TIME: 30 minutes • **YIELD:** about 1 pound (454 g)

INGREDIENTS

1 cup (158 g) rice flour
1 cup (120 g) tapioca starch
2 cups (475 ml) water
½ tsp salt
2 tsp vegetable oil

In Vietnam, we seldom use dried pho noodles sold in packets at the supermarket; instead, we use fresh noodles (*bánh phở*) that are available at local markets at a very low cost. Traditionally, noodles are made by soaking uncooked rice overnight in water to soften. The rice is then ground up and mixed with tapioca starch to get a white batter. The batter is then ladled and spread on a piece of cloth stretched over a steaming pot. The heated mixture hardens in a few minutes to form a white and delicate rice sheet. It is then lifted with a long bamboo stick and placed on a bamboo mat to dry. Once the surface is no longer tacky, the sheets are stacked and cut into noodle strips.

It is difficult to replicate the traditional process at home, unless you can get ahold of a specialized steamer for rice sheet making. (They do sell this kind of steamer at local markets in Vietnam, which is normally used to make Vietnamese steamed rice rolls (*bánh cuốn*). The following method is for making noodles at home with simple kitchenware.

INSTRUCTIONS

1. Combine all ingredients in a large bowl and stir well. Let the batter rest for 1 to 2 hours.

2. Place a plate on the steaming rack in a steamer. Steam the plate for 1 to 2 minutes, or until hot.

3. Stir the batter and ladle just enough batter to cover the base of the plate. Steam for 4 to 5 minutes, until set and quite translucent.

4. Run a spatula around the edges of the rice noodle sheet and carefully peel it off the plate. Transfer to a flat surface to cool. Repeat with remaining batter.

5. Stack 2 or 3 rice sheets on top of each other when done and sheets are cooled. Cut into noodle strips to the thickness desired.

HOW TO COOK DRIED NOODLES

SKILL LEVEL: Easy • **PREP TIME:** 10 minutes
COOK TIME: 10 minutes • **YIELD:** 3 pounds (1.1 kg) cooked noodles

INGREDIENTS

12 cups (2½ qt, or 2.5 L) water
1 tbsp (15 ml) vinegar
1 tsp vegetable oil
17½-oz (500 g) package dried
  noodles

COOKING TIP

You can soak the dried noodles in water for 5 minutes before boiling. This helps to reduce the cooking time.

To help reduce clumping, place a bowl facedown in a strainer and then drain the noodles over it. The round shape of the bowl prevents the noodles from forming into a solid block, making it easier to fluff and separate them.

If you are unable to make or buy fresh pho noodles, dried noodles work just as well. This cooking method applies to many kinds of dried noodles including *bánh phở,* *bún,* *hủ tiếu dai,* **and** *mì Quảng.* *Miến* **are prepared differently so follow the package instructions.**

INSTRUCTIONS

1. Bring a large saucepan of water to a boil. Add the vinegar and vegetable oil. (The vinegar helps keep the noodles in shape and the oil prevents sticking.)

2. Add the dried noodles to the saucepan and boil for 5 to 10 minutes, following package instructions. Remove the noodles from the heat when they are soft but still a bit chewy (al dente).

3. Drain and rinse under cold water to remove the starch outside the noodles and stop the cooking process.

4. Rinse again with hot water to help the noodles dry out faster and reduce clumping. (This second rinse with hot water helps the moisture to evaporate more quickly. The noodles will stay dry and firm. If you skip this step, you might end up with soggy noodles that later form into a cake.)

RICE NOODLE DIRECTORY

GLASS NOODLE (*miến*)

TAPIOCA (*hủ tiếu dai*)

PHO (*bánh phở*)

RICE VERMICELLI (*bún*)

EGG (*mì Quảng*)

WHAT TO SERVE WITH PHO

Now that your perfect bowl of pho is almost ready, here are the fresh herbs, condiments, and more that you can serve with it to help enhance its flavor even more. You can choose any or all of these items. It's up to you!

- Thinly sliced yellow onion
- Chopped green scallion
- White part of scallion (This is a signature item in an authentic bowl of pho. Quickly smash with the side of a knife and blanch for only two seconds in the broth. This small detail will show how serious you are about pho!)
- Few sprigs Asian basil
- Few sprigs sawtooth herb
- Few sprigs mint, rice paddy herb, or Vietnamese mint (Though some pho joints do serve this with pho, I strongly believe the only two herbs to use in pho are Asian basil and sawtooth herb.)
- Blanched bean sprouts
- Lime wedges
- Thinly sliced bird's eye chili peppers
- Pickled Garlic (page 164)
- Chili Jam (page 162)
- Fish sauce
- Hoisin sauce*
- Sriracha*

COOKING TIP

In northern Vietnam, pho never comes with hoisin sauce, bean sprouts, or fresh herbs; it is garnished simply with some chopped scallion and a sprinkle of black pepper. A few jars of additional condiments, such as fish sauce, chili jam, and pickled garlic are found on the table.

*By squeezing hoisin sauce and sriracha into every bowl of pho you eat, you do a disservice to all pho restaurants. You lose your chance to treasure the flavor that the chefs spent hours to achieve and years of experience to perfect. The best way to enjoy pho is to eat half a bowl first to enjoy the unique flavors it has to offer, and then add these extras. This way, you know which pho shops offer the soup most pleasing to your palate.

HOW TO BUILD A BOWL OF PHO

The pho bowl in Vietnam is rather small compared to the one offered in restaurants in Europe and the United States. Sometimes it is as small as half the size as in the United States. Please keep this in mind when you read the yield size of the recipes.

Your broth has simmered to perfection and your toppings and garnishes are prepped. Now what? It's time to assemble the perfect bowl of pho! Once you are able to orchestrate the timing of everything to deliver a proper bowl that has all of the elements working together, these skills can then be transferred to any bowl that you build going forward. Follow these easy steps and you'll have a bowl that will make you (and others) satisfied.

1. Bring a large saucepan filled with water to a boil.

2. Add the bean sprouts to the saucepan and blanch for 3 to 5 seconds.

3. Place a handful of noodles (fresh or cooked dried noodles) in a long-handle noodle strainer and blanch for 5 to 10 seconds. When you lift up the strainer, let the hot water drip into the empty bowl. Give the bowl a swirl and pour out the hot water. The noodles and bowl are then warmed up, ready for the hot soup.

4. Place the warmed noodles in the bowl.

5. Add toppings such as sliced meat, chopped scallion, and sliced onion to the bowl.

6. Smash the white part of the scallion and blanch in the broth for 2 seconds. Ladle the scallion and hot soup over the noodles.

7. Add additional garnishes such as fresh herbs, blanched bean sprouts, sliced chili peppers, and a squeeze of lime.

8. Enjoy!

Phở Vidéo

20 Kg xương bò 4 Kg plat de côtes 1 Kg → 2 Kg hành củ gừng tươi, cỡ bằng bàn tay 1² → 25 bông hoa hồi 2 - 3 → 6 trái thảo quả 4 → 8 cái nu đinh 1½ → 3 miếng quế khô cỡ ngón tay út	Nếu nấu dưới 10 Kg xương và 2 Kg plat de côtes, thì tôi khuyên không nên nấu phở. (Phải 8 tiếng đồng hồ).

1½ → 3 Kg hành củ ngò gai hành lá rau quế rau ngò chanh ớt bánh phở tươi thịt tái rumsteak	Ăn xong, còn dư nước lèo, nhớ hâm sôi lại, đừng bị hư. Lửa sôi tắt liền, đừng để bị đục nước lèo.	Xương: xương gân + xương đầu gối + xương tủy, đừng khi nào nấu xương tủy không. Sau khi vớt thịt chín ra, cho thêm vào nồi 1 hay 2 lít nước.

Nấu nồi nước to cho sôi. Bỏ 4 Kg plat de côtes vào, cho ngập nước trên miếng thịt, trần sơ cho sôi 10 phút, sau vớt ra để một bên. Cho xương vào, để sôi. Lại nhỏ lửa xuống 20 phút sau, vớt xương, rửa cho sạch. (Hớt nước mỡ ở trên để vào một cái soong. Sau đó, để xương vào một cái nồi (thật to) Đổ vào 30 lít nước, nấu lên cho sôi. Nhỏ lửa riu riu. (Đừng cho sôi to, nước lèo sẽ đục).

ORIGINAL PHO BÒ RECIPE BY PHO VIDÉO

I acquired this recipe from a legendary pho restaurant in Paris. It makes enough to feed a small army, but I thought it would be special and unique to include the history of this restaurant and the recipe in this book. For a simplified beef pho soup recipe, see page 44.

Recipes are the most precious assets of any restaurant, and that's especially true in a pho restaurant. Even when you're friends with the owners, it's not easy to get their special recipe.

Stefan Leistner, author of the German cookbook *Asia Street Food*, is a good friend of mine. We met in Hamburg and several times in Da Nang and Hoi An, where he travels every year to learn about Vietnamese food. At a cookbook fair in Paris, he met Thierry Bertman, who shared this recipe from Pho Vidéo, handwritten in Vietnamese. Pho Vidéo had the facade of a video store, but illegally sold pho instead. Stefan and Thierry longed to have an English translation of the recipe, and that's how I came to see it.

As I read the recipe, I imagined it must have been written out by a meticulous and passionate yet grumpy chef/owner, because he also went into details that sounded like him nagging a kitchen assistant: "Do not pour the skimmed fat into the sink as it might block the drainage. Let it cool and throw it in the trash the next day."

Since I really wanted to share this recipe in *Simply Pho*, I needed to find the recipe owner to ask permission. I googled "Pho Vidéo" and "Pho Vidéo restaurant," but no luck. All that popped up in the search results were some videos on how to cook pho (including my popular tutorial on YouTube!). Luckily, I found Stefan, who was in Hoi An for a few weeks with his entire family to celebrate the wedding of his son, but he didn't know who had written the recipe either. We didn't know whether the restaurant was even still open.

It came to me that, since it's supposed to be such a famous restaurant in Paris, there might be some good information in French. So I asked a favor of Huynh Thien Luong, a friend of mine in Paris, and she found the most valuable info in French on *Kha's Blog*. My cousin Le Thao Nguyen, who once studied in France, helped me translate. You can't believe how happy I was to finally find the origin of the recipe!

NOTES

- Warm up your leftover broth by bringing it to a boil. Then turn off the heat right away. Otherwise the broth will turn cloudy.

- Use a mix of bones, not just marrow. Beef ribs are crucial for a tasty broth.

- After removing the meat, add 4 to 8 cups (1 to 2 quarts, or 1 to 2 L) of water.

- If the noodles are overcooked and sticky after blanching, rinse under cold water, then blanch again in hot water (for 1 second).

- Do not leave the onion and sawtooth herb in the broth for more than 45 minutes. Remove and add another batch, if any.

- Skim off the fat, if any. Do not pour the skimmed fat into the sink as it will block the drainage. Let it cool and throw in the trash on the next day.

According to Kha Tran's blog, Pho Vidéo was located on rue Claude-Bernard, and served the best and most expensive pho in France's capital. The shop with only a dozen seats was open for over ten years in the 1990s and operated in complete secrecy behind shelves of videos—the pho maker had hijacked the lease of a video rental shop.

Despite the growing success of his restaurant, the grumpy, old Vietnamese owner would absolutely not expand his business: He just wanted to pay for his son to go to medical school and buy him a doctor's office. He would only serve a certain number of pho bowls each day, five days a week, and he did not accept reservations, which made his fans crave his pho even more. It was common for people who had traveled an hour to Pho Video to hear "There's nothing left." When frustrated patrons asked him to open more often, he threatened *to close* one more day a week!

As if he anticipated closing the restaurant, one day, he began sharing his special recipe. Many copies have circulated among his fans; I probably translated a copy of one. I was so sad to learn that the legendary Pho Vidéo was indeed closed due to the death of the owner. Since he decided to share his recipe with the public, I don't think he would have minded me publishing it in a cookbook to spread the word about his phenomenal pho to many more generations.

One thing a lot of people are concerned about when they eat pho, no matter how much they love it, is the level of MSG in the soup. I dare say that all pho shops, in Vietnam and overseas, famous or not, do use MSG in making the broth, and probably a lot of it. It's hard to cook tasty pho without it. But when you read this Pho Video recipe, you'll understand what it takes to go without MSG. For twenty servings, he used 44 pounds (20 kg) of beef bones and 9 pounds (4 kg) of beef ribs, then another 4½ pounds (2 kg) of onions. If that didn't make the soup tasty enough, I don't know what would. No wonder his pho was so good and expensive!

Here is the direct translation of the recipe. You can halve the recipe, but no further. If you use less than 22 pounds (10 kg) of beef bones and 4½ pounds (2 kg) of beef ribs, you'd better NOT cook this pho. It has to be cooked for at least 8 hours.

SKILL LEVEL: Advanced • **PREP TIME:** 1 hour • **COOK TIME:** 9 to 11 hours • **YIELD:** 20 servings

INGREDIENTS

9 lb (4 kg) beef ribs
44 lb (20 kg) beef bones
6¾ lb (3 kg) onions, divided
1 hand-size piece of ginger, plus 3 slices ginger (cut into ⅛-inch-thick, or 3 mm, slices)
6 black cardamom pods
3 cinnamon sticks
8 cloves
25 star anise
½ cup plus 2 tbsp (150 ml) fish sauce, plus more to taste
2 tbsp (30 ml) salt, plus more to taste
1 tbsp (15 ml) black pepper, plus a few pinches, divided
Rumpsteak (for rare beef)
Scallions
Cilantro
Asian basil
Sawtooth herb
Few pinches MSG
Fresh pho noodles
Lime
Chili peppers

COOKING TIP

If using 44 pounds (20 kg) of bones, you'll need a pot that is at least 16½ to 17½ inches (42 to 45 cm) in diameter. For 22 pounds (10 kg) of bones, you'll need a pot that is at least 13 to 13¾ inches (33 to 35 cm) in diameter.

INSTRUCTIONS

1. Bring a large pot of water to a boil. Add the beef ribs, making sure they are fully covered with water. Parboil the beef ribs for 10 minutes, then remove and set aside. Add the beef bones to the pot and boil over low heat for 20 minutes. Remove the bones and rinse well. Skim the fat and set aside to discard of properly later.

2. Transfer the ribs and bones to a large pot filled with 8 gallons (30 L) of water. Bring to a boil and reduce the heat to low. (Do not cook over high heat as it will make the broth less clear.)

3. Halve 4½ pounds (2 kg) of onions and char for 3 minutes. Smash the piece of ginger and add it to the pot, along with the charred onions, black cardamom pods, cinnamon sticks, cloves, star anise, ½ cup plus 2 tablespoons (150 ml) fish sauce, 2 tablespoons salt (30 ml), and 1 tablespoon (15 ml) black pepper.

4. Bring to a boil and cook over very low heat for 2 to 3 hours. When the beef ribs are tender, remove and set aside. Also remove the ginger, onions, and spices. Keep simmering over low heat for 8 to 10 hours.

5. Strain the broth into another large pot. Bring to a boil again and immediately turn off the heat. Let it sit until the next day.

6. Thinly slice the rumpsteak and the beef ribs. Chop the scallions and thinly slice the onions for serving into rings. Finely chop the cilantro, Asian basil, and sawtooth herb.

7. Before serving, bring the broth to a boil. Add 2¼ pounds (1 kg) of the onion slices, a few sawtooth herb sprigs, 3 slices ginger, and a few pinches each of black pepper and MSG. (You won't need much MSG as the onion is already sweet.) Add fish sauce and salt to taste.

8. Blanch the pho noodles in a large pot of water (a big pot helps fluff the noodles).

9. Place noodles in a serving bowl, add the sliced beef, and ladle the soup over. Drain and pour the soup back into the pot.

10. Add sliced onion and chopped scallion to the bowl. Ladle the soup over. Arrange the rare rumpsteak on top. Top with the chopped herbs. Serve with the limes and chili peppers.

APPETIZERS

Khai vị

FRESH SPRING ROLLS

SKILL LEVEL: Easy • **PREP TIME:** 30 minutes • **COOK TIME:** 45 minutes • **YIELD:** 15 rolls

INGREDIENTS

Spring Rolls

10½ oz (300 g) pork belly

1 tsp salt

7 oz (200 g) shrimp (about 15 total)

7 oz (200 g) rice vermicelli noodles
   (*bún*)

Fresh greens and herbs such as
   lettuce, mint, cilantro,and perilla,

1 cucumber, cut into 3 x 1-inch
   (7 x 2.5 cm) lengths

15 rice paper wrappers (8½ inch,
   or 22 cm, in diameter)

5 garlic chives, cut into 4-inch
   (20 cm) lengths (optional)

Dipping Sauce

1 tbsp (15 ml) vegetable oil

1 tbsp (10 g) minced garlic

5 tbsp (80 g) hoisin sauce

1 tbsp (16 g) peanut butter

1 tbsp (15 ml) sugar

1 tsp minced bird's eye chili
   pepper

1 tbsp (9 g) crushed roasted
   peanuts

SHOPPING TIP

To reduce fat, replace the pork
belly with pork loin or pork
shoulder.

Refreshing, light, and full of flavor, fresh spring rolls (*gỏi cuốn*) are one of Vietnam's world-famous dishes. The dipping sauce is what makes all the difference; the richness of the peanut butter complements the sweet tanginess of the hoisin sauce. This particular version comes from the South. In Vietnam, these are street snacks, while most Vietnamese restaurants overseas serve them as an appetizer. It's fun to let everyone around the table make their own rolls. Learning the skill of rolling is a great way to experience Vietnamese dining culture. This also saves you the task of rolling yourself!

INSTRUCTIONS

1. **To make the rolls:** Fill a medium saucepan half-full with water and bring to a rolling boil. Add the pork belly and salt.

2. Bring to a boil again, then reduce the heat to medium and cook for 25 to 35 minutes, depending on the thickness of the pork cut. To test the pork, pierce the meat with a chopstick or fork and when the water coming out runs clear, not pink, it's cooked through. Remove the pork and soak in cold water for 5 minutes to prevent it from darkening. Drain and let cool. Reserve the broth for later use.

3. In a large pan, cook the shrimp, without oil, over medium heat for 1 to 2 minutes, until they turn orange. Let cool and peel. Slice each shrimp in half lengthwise. Remove any black lines running through the shrimp meat.

4. Cook the rice vermicelli noodles in boiling water for 3 to 5 minutes, until soft (or follow package instructions). Drain and rinse the noodles under cold water to stop the cooking.

5. **To make the dipping sauce:** Heat the vegetable oil in a small pan over medium-high heat. Add the garlic and fry until golden brown. Add the hoisin sauce, 5 tablespoons (75 ml) of the reserved pork broth, peanut butter, and sugar to the pan. Stir well and simmer over low heat for 1 to 2 minutes, until slightly thickened. Pour the sauce into condiment bowls and top with the minced chili peppers and crushed peanuts.

continued on page 32

6. **To assemble the rolls:** Place the cooked noodles, shrimp, pork, fresh greens, and sliced cucumber on plates. Prepare a pan of lukewarm water to soften the rice paper and find a flat work surface (like a cutting board or large plate) for the rolling job.

7. Dip one piece of rice paper into the water, covering the paper with water without soaking it. Gently shake off the excess water and lay it on the flat surface.

8. Place the fresh vegetables in a row, from left to right, on the lower third of the rice paper wrappers, leaving about 2 inches (5 cm) on both sides. Next, place some noodles, cucumber slices, 2 pork slices, and 2 shrimp halves on the rice paper, in rows parallel to the vegetables. Keep the orange sides of the shrimp facing down.

9. Starting from the end closest to the filling, roll once or twice until you reach the center of the rice paper. Fold the left and right sides inward, and continue rolling. You can also add a garlic chive at the end to give the roll a little "tail." Repeat these steps for the remaining 14 rolls.

10. To serve, either spoon some dipping sauce onto the rolls or dip them into the sauce. You can also cut the rolls diagonally in half to make them more manageable to eat. Serve the rolls within 2 hours of wrapping. (If you are going on a picnic, you can wrap the rolls in plastic to keep them fresh for a few hours longer. This will prevent the rice paper from drying out and becoming sticky.)

COMBO SALAD

SKILL LEVEL: Easy • **PREP TIME:** 20 minutes • **COOK TIME:** 45 minutes • **YIELD:** 4 servings

INGREDIENTS

3½ oz (100 g) medium shrimp

3½ oz (100 g) pork belly or chicken breast

1 tsp salt

2 tbsp (30 ml) fish sauce

2 tbsp (30 ml) sugar

2 tbsp (30 ml) fresh lime juice

2 tsp combined minced garlic and chili peppers

7 oz (200 g) cucumber, core removed and julienned

7 oz (200 g) carrot, julienned

3½ oz (100 g) lotus stem or daikon, julienned

3½ oz (100 g) banana blossom or red cabbage, shredded

3½ oz (100 g) red onion or red bell pepper, julienned

3½ oz (100 g) shredded beef jerky or shredded dried squid

3 tbsp (24 g) roasted sesame seeds

¼ cup (36 g) crushed roasted peanuts

16 prawn crackers or 3 large sesame crackers, for serving

This salad (*gỏi thập cẩm*) is a common appetizer for weddings and housewarming parties, as it is pleasing to the eye yet easy to make. The ingredient list is very flexible: Use whatever salad ingredients are in season. Just make sure you have a good variety of color and texture, and your platter will tempt all the senses. The mixing should be done at the table, so the salad is fresh and not watery.

INSTRUCTIONS

1. Steam the shrimp for 3 to 5 minutes, until the color changes to orange. Then peel, devein, and slice each shrimp in half lengthwise.

2. Place the pork belly in a medium saucepan and fill with enough water to cover it. Add the 1 teaspoon salt, bring to a boil, and cook over medium-low heat until done, about 30 minutes. When you poke the meat with a chopstick or skewer and the water coming out runs clear, not pink, it is cooked. Let cool and thinly slice.

3. To make the vinaigrette, in a small bowl, combine the fish sauce, sugar, and lime juice. Stir well to dissolve the sugar. Add the minced garlic and chili peppers last to keep them afloat on top.

4. Arrange all the julienned vegetables on a serving platter together with the shredded beef jerky, pork, and shrimp. Place the bowl of vinaigrette in the center of the platter.

5. To serve, pour the vinaigrette over the salad and mix well. Garnish with roasted sesame seeds and crushed peanuts. Serve on top of prawn or sesame crackers like bruschetta.

BEEF SHANK SALAD

SKILL LEVEL: Easy • **PREP TIME:** 20 minutes • **COOK TIME:** 30 minutes • **YIELD:** 6 to 8 servings

INGREDIENTS

10½ oz (300 g) yellow or red onion, peeled and thinly sliced

2 tbsp (30 ml) white vinegar

4 tbsp (50 g) sugar, divided

2 lb (907 g) whole beef shank

1 double-thumb-size knob ginger, peeled, divided

3 cloves garlic

2 bird's eye chili peppers

¼ cup (60 ml) fish sauce

2 cups (60 g) chopped mint leaves

⅓ cup (48 g) crushed roasted peanuts

20 prawn crackers, for serving (optional)

To really enjoy this salad (*gỏi bắp bò*), it is important to cook the beef shank just long enough. While most Western recipes require two to three hours to cook this cut, the Vietnamese prefer a slightly chewier texture. As soon as you cut into the meat and the liquid runs clear, it's time to take it out. It will be done but still firm, so you can slice it very thin—the classic way to prepare this dish. The pickled onion adds just the right tanginess.

INSTRUCTIONS

1. Add the onion, vinegar, and 2 tablespoons (25 g) of the sugar to a large bowl. Mix well and let sit for 30 minutes.

2. Place the beef shank in a pressure cooker or stockpot and fill with just enough water to cover it. Bring to a boil.

3. Smash one-third of the ginger and add to the pressure cooker or pot. When it boils again, reduce the heat to low and cover with the lid. Cook for 15 to 20 minutes in the pressure cooker, depending on the size of the beef shank. If using a stockpot, cook the beef until it is fork-tender, 40 to 50 minutes.

4. Let the pressure cooker cool down completely before opening the lid. Remove the beef shank and let cool. Cut into very thin slices against the grain.

5. In a mortar and pestle, crush the remaining ginger, garlic, and chili peppers into a very fine paste. In a medium bowl, combine the paste with the fish sauce and remaining 2 tablespoons (25 g) sugar. Stir well to dissolve. Set aside one-third of this dressing to serve as a dipping sauce.

6. Squeeze out the excess liquid from the pickled onion and combine with the beef in a large bowl. Add a few tablespoons of dressing and toss well. Taste and adjust with additional dressing to your liking.

7. Toss with the mint leaves and crushed peanuts, saving some peanuts for garnish.

8. Transfer to a serving platter. Top with the remaining crushed peanuts and serve with the prawn crackers.

VIETNAMESE CRÊPES

SKILL LEVEL: Intermediate • **PREP TIME:** 30 minutes • **COOK TIME:** 30 minutes • **YIELD:** 4 to 6 servings

INGREDIENTS

2⅔ cups (400 g) rice flour

2 tsp turmeric powder

1 tsp salt, plus more to taste

2¼ cups (535 ml) water

1 cup (235 ml) beer, club soda, or coconut milk

3 scallions, chopped

1 lb (454 g) small white shrimp, tips and legs trimmed

10½ oz (300 g) pork belly, thinly sliced

Black pepper, to taste

Vegetable oil, for frying

1 lb (454 g) bean sprouts

Lettuce or mustard leaves (optional)

20 rice paper wrappers, softened with water (optional)

Fresh herbs such as mint, cilantro, and perilla

Fish Sauce Dressing (page 167), for serving

COOKING TIPS

- Use a heavy frying pan with a thick bottom; cast iron works best.
- Add more cooking oil (to equal 2 to 3 tablespoons, or 30 to 45 ml) for each crêpe.
- The small bubbles in beer and club soda make a lighter batter.
- Blend some day-old cooked rice into the batter.
- Fry twice: For the first fry, make all the crêpes and stack them on top of each other. For the second fry, add the bean sprouts.

When it's cold and rainy, don't you crave warm, filling food? Vietnamese crêpes (*bánh xèo*) are perfect for those moody days. Making *bánh xèo* might look easy, but turning out a perfect crispy crêpe is a tricky business. See Cooking Tips (below left) for some of the tricks I've learned after making crêpes hundreds of times.

INSTRUCTIONS

1. In a large bowl, dissolve the rice flour, turmeric powder, and 1 teaspoon salt in the water.

2. Add the beer and chopped scallion to the bowl. Stir well and let the batter rest for 30 minutes.

3. Season the shrimp and pork belly with salt and black pepper. Set aside.

4. Heat an 8-inch (20 cm) heavy-bottomed or cast-iron pan over medium-high heat. Add 2 to 3 tablespoons (30 to 45 ml) vegetable oil. Add 2 shrimp and a few pork slices, and cook until the shrimp and pork change color on both sides.

5. Ladle about ⅓ cup (80 ml) of the batter into the pan and tilt in a circular motion to spread the batter evenly. Cover the pan and cook for 1 minute. Uncover and add some bean sprouts, then cover again and cook for another minute.

6. Fold the crêpe in half so that the 2 shrimp stay on opposite sides. Cook for another minute, uncovered, and transfer to a plate. Repeat until you finish the batter, making sure there is 2 to 3 tablespoons (35 to 40 ml) of vegetable oil in the pan for frying each crêpe. If you can manage 2 to 3 pans at a time, the process will go faster.

7. To serve, use scissors to cut the crêpe in half crosswise. Take a large piece of lettuce or softened rice paper wrapper, and place some herbs and half of a crêpe on top.

8. Roll it up, dip it in the Fish Sauce Dressing, and enjoy.

RARE BEEF IN LIME JUICE SALAD

SKILL LEVEL: Easy • **PREP TIME:** 20 minutes • **COOK TIME:** 1 minute • **YIELD:** 4 to 6 servings

INGREDIENTS

2 medium red or yellow onions, thinly sliced

3 tbsp (45 ml) rice vinegar

3 tbsp (38 g) sugar, divided

1 lb (454 g) beef (eye of round or sirloin), thinly sliced against the grain

½ tsp salt

½ tsp black pepper

½ tsp chicken stock powder

Juice of 4 limes

3 tbsp (45 ml) vegetable oil

1 head garlic, minced

1 cup (30 g) chopped mint

1 cup (30 g) chopped rice paddy herb

1 cup (30 g) chopped sawtooth herb

2 tbsp (18 g) crushed roasted peanuts

2 tbsp (20 g) crispy fried shallot (*hành phi*; you can buy these at an Asian food store)

2 red chili peppers, thinly sliced on the bias

Prawn crackers or sesame rice crackers, for serving

Anchovy Dipping Sauce (page 168) or soy sauce, for serving

This dish (*bò tái chanh*) is similar to the Italian dish carpaccio, in which thin slices of beef are served raw or rare on top of a bed of greens. It is perfect to serve as an appetizer or with drinks. This is normally served with prawn crackers and a bowl of Anchovy Dipping Sauce (page 168).

INSTRUCTIONS

1. Soak the onion slices in ice water for 10 minutes. Drain and mix with the vinegar and 2 tablespoons (25 g) of the sugar. Set aside.

2. Season the beef with the salt, black pepper, and chicken stock powder, and the remaining 1 tablespoon (13 g) sugar. Let sit for 10 minutes.

3. Place the beef in a large bowl with the lime juice. Let sit for 15 to 20 minutes. The acid in the citrus will "cook" the beef, turning it pale in color.

4. Heat the vegetable oil in a medium pan over medium heat. Add the garlic and fry until golden brown. Pour over the beef and mix well.

5. To assemble the dish, arrange the fresh herbs on a large serving platter. Top with the pickled onions, followed by the rare beef in lime juice.

6. Garnish with the crushed peanuts, fried shallot, and chili pepper slices. Serve with the prawn crackers and Anchovy Dipping Sauce.

SHOPPING TIP

As the beef is not cooked, it is crucial to choose very fresh, high-quality beef from a butcher you trust.

VEGAN GREEN SPRING ROLLS

SKILL LEVEL: Intermediate • **PREP TIME:** 1 hour • **COOK TIME:** 15 minutes • **YIELD:** 20 rolls

INGREDIENTS

Spring Rolls

2 tbsp (30 ml) vegetable oil, plus more for frying

10½ oz (300 g) tofu, cut into ½-inch-thick (13 mm) steaks and wrapped in paper towels to remove the moisture

1 medium carrot, julienned, divided

1½ tsp sugar, divided

1 tbsp (15 ml) rice vinegar

1 tbsp (6 g) minced scallion (white part only), plus 10 scallions (green parts only and kept whole), divided

2 oz (56 g) dried woodear mushrooms, soaked in hot water for 15 minutes, drained, excess water squeezed out, and cut into ¼-inch-thick (6 mm) strips

1 tsp mushroom seasoning powder, divided

¼ tsp salt

2 small sweet potatoes, peeled, steamed, and cut into sticks the size of French fries

3½ oz (100 g) vegan ham, cut into sticks the size of French fries

3½ oz (100 g) fresh herbs such as mint, basil, and perilla

7 oz (200 g) fresh or cooked rice vermicelli noodles

1 lb (454 g) mustard greens, rinsed

Besides the rolling technique, the dipping sauce is the key to the success of these spring rolls (*cuốn diếp chay*). Fermented soybean sauce is sold at Asian food stores under the name of *tương bần*, *tương Bắc*, or *tương Cự Đà*. It is pungent and very bold in flavor, which helps to enhance the flavor of vegan dishes.

INSTRUCTIONS

1. **To make the spring roll filling:** Place a large pan over medium heat. Fill with vegetable oil to a depth of 1 inch (2.5 cm). Heat until the oil reaches 360°F (180°C), or test the temperature with a chopstick inserted into the oil: when bubbles appear around the chopstick, the oil is ready for deep-frying. Gently slide in the tofu steaks and fry until golden brown on both sides. Remove and place on a paper towel–lined plate to drain the excess oil. Let cool completely and cut lengthwise into long, ¼-inch-thick (6 mm) sticks.

2. In a medium bowl, combine half of the carrot with the 1 teaspoon of the sugar and the vinegar. Mix well and set aside.

3. Heat 2 tablespoons (30 ml) vegetable oil in a large wok or pan over medium heat. Add the minced scallion and cook and stir until golden brown. Add the remaining carrot and cook and stir for 1 to 2 minutes, until soft.

4. Add the woodear mushrooms, the remaining ½ teaspoon sugar, ½ teaspoon of the mushroom seasoning powder, and the salt to the wok. Stir well and cook for 1 minute. Add the tofu and toss to combine. Remove from the heat and let cool.

5. Bring a medium saucepan of water to a rolling boil. Quickly blanch the green parts of the 10 scallions for 30 seconds, or until wilted. Transfer to a large bowl filled with ice water to stop the cooking process and maintain the green color. Drain and set aside.

6. **To assemble the rolls:** Place the stir-fry, sweet potatoes, vegan ham, fresh herbs, noodles, mustard greens, and green scallions on plates. Find a flat work surface (like a cutting board or large plate) for the rolling job.

Dipping Sauce

1 tbsp (15 ml) vegetable oil
1 tbsp (6 g) minced scallion (white part only)
¼ cup (60 g) fermented soybean sauce (*tương bần or tương Cự Đà*)
4 tsp sugar
1 tbsp (16 g) peanut butter
½ cup (120 ml) water
¼ cup (32 g) roasted sesame seeds
1 tsp minced bird's eye chili peppers

SHOPPING TIP

"Mustard greens" (*Brassica juncea*) is a very generic term for a variety of plants that differ sharply in heat, flavor, and appearance. The kind used in this recipe is called *cải cay* or *cải bẹ xanh* in Vietnamese or *juk gai choy* in Cantonese. It is leafy and a light romaine green. The slim stems are also light green, generally narrow, celery-shaped, and pretty juicy. The leaves are slightly ruffled, somewhat narrow, and lettuce-like, and have a remarkable mustard nip. Due to its superior flavor, it's often eaten fresh in place of lettuce in certain Vietnamese dishes. You can get it in the fresh vegetable section at Asian food stores.

7. Remove the thick part of the mustard leaf stems. Place one leaf on the flat surface with the dark side facing down. Place a bit of each filling ingredient—stir-fry, sweet potatoes, vegan ham, fresh herbs, and noodles—on top and roll it up. Use one leaf peeled from a blanched scallion as a string to tie up the roll nicely. Repeat with the remaining mustard leaves, fillings, and scallions. Place the rolls parallel to each other and trim off the top and bottom edges to make them uniform in size.

8. **To make the dipping sauce:** Heat the vegetable oil in a small pan over medium heat. Add the minced scallion and cook and stir until fragrant. Add the fermented soybean sauce, sugar, peanut butter, and water to the pan. Stir well and simmer for 1 to 2 minutes, until smooth and thickened. Transfer to a serving bowl. Add the roasted sesame seeds and mix well. Top with the minced chili peppers for more heat and color.

9. To serve, either spoon some dipping sauce onto the rolls or dip them into the sauce.

PHO NOODLE SOUPS

Các món phở nước

SIMPLIFIED PHO NOODLE SOUP WITH BEEF

SKILL LEVEL: Intermediate • **PREP TIME:** 30 minutes • **COOK TIME:** 2 to 8 hours • **YIELD:** 8 to 10 servings

INGREDIENTS

Broth

5 lb (2.2 kg) beef bones (marrow and knuckle)
1 lb (454 g) beef brisket or flank, kept whole
20 cups (5 qt, or 5 L) water
1 medium yellow onion, peeled
1 tbsp (15 ml) salt, plus more to taste
1 thumb-size piece rock sugar, plus more to taste
Chicken stock powder, to taste

Pho Aroma

1 medium yellow onion, unpeeled and halved
2 thumb-size knobs ginger, cut lengthwise into ⅛-inch-thick (3 mm) slices
3 star anise
2 cinnamon sticks
2 or 3 black cardamom pods
1 tsp cloves (optional)
1 tsp coriander seeds (optional)

While traditional *phở bò* **takes at least eight hours to cook, this is a simpler version you can cook in your home kitchen, and the result will be just as satisfying.**

INSTRUCTIONS

1. **To make the broth:** Place the beef bones in a stockpot filled with enough water to cover them. Bring to a boil and cook for 5 to 10 minutes, until the impurities rise to the top. Drain the pot and rinse the bones well under running water to wash away the impurities.

2. Place the bones in a large stockpot with the beef brisket and the water. (If you use the same pot as in step 1, make sure you clean it before putting the bones back. It is crucial for a clear broth.) Add the onion, 1 tablespoon (15 ml) salt, and thumb-size piece rock sugar to the stockpot. Bring to a boil, reduce the heat to low, and simmer, uncovered. Occasionally skim off the scum. Depending on the cut of beef, it might take 1 to 2 hours to cook. If the broth reduces, add hot water to compensate, making sure you always have the same amount as when you started.

3. **To make the pho aroma:** Heat the onion halves and ginger slices directly over an open flame on the stove until slightly charred on all sides. Peel the grilled onion, but try to keep the stem intact and not let the onion layers fall apart. Rinse the onion and ginger under warm running water and scrape off the charred bits.

4. Toast the star anise, cinnamon sticks, black cardamom pods, cloves (if using), and coriander seeds (if using) in a large pan over medium-low heat until fragrant, about 2 minutes. Place these spices in a spice ball or large tea or spice bag(s), or wrap in a piece of cheesecloth. Add the spices and the charred onion and ginger into the stockpot 30 to 45 minutes before serving, so the aroma stays fresh and tempting.

continued on page 46

Pho Bowl

3⅓ lb (1.5 kg) fresh or cooked pho noodles

10½ oz (300 g) beef (eye of round or sirloin), thinly sliced against the grain

1 small or medium yellow onion, sliced very thin, soaked in ice water for 15 minutes, and drained

3 to 5 scallions (green parts chopped; white parts kept whole, smashed, and blanched)

3 sprigs Asian basil

3 sprigs sawtooth herb

1 lb (454 g) bean sprouts, blanched (optional)

1 lime, cut into wedges

Hoisin sauce (optional)

Sriracha (optional)

5. When you pierce the meat with a chopstick and see no pink water coming out, it is cooked. Remove and soak in a large bowl of cold water for 5 minutes to prevent the beef from drying up or turning dark. Drain and thinly slice into bite-size pieces. Set aside.

6. Remove the onion halves from the stockpot before they break, which will make the broth less clear. Continue to simmer the broth for at least a few more hours on very low heat if you have time. The broth should simmer for at least 2 hours from the beginning of making the recipe and up to 8 hours. If the broth reduces, add hot water to compensate, making sure you always have the same amount as when you started.

7. Season the broth to taste with salt, sugar, and stock powder.

8. **To assemble the pho bowls:** Fill each serving bowl one-third full with noodles (about a handful of noodles). Top with sliced beef (cooked and/or raw beef, your choice), onion slices, chopped scallions, and blanched scallions.

9. Ladle the hot broth over the noodles to fill the bowl. The broth will cook the raw beef in seconds.

10. Serve with a platter of the fresh herbs, blanched bean sprouts, and lime wedges, along with the hoisin sauce and sriracha, if using these condiments.

PHO NOODLE SOUP WITH CHICKEN

SKILL LEVEL: Intermediate • **PREP TIME:** 20 minutes • **COOK TIME:** 1 hour 15 minutes • **YIELD:** 8 to 10 servings

INGREDIENTS

Broth

1 tbsp (15 ml) salt, plus more to taste

1 whole chicken (about 2.5 lb, or 1.2 kg)

1 scallion

2 slices ginger (cut lengthwise into ⅛-inch-thick, or 3 mm, slices)

16 cups (4 qt, or 4 L) water

1 tsp chicken stock powder, plus more to taste (optional)

1 medium yellow onion, peeled

1 tsp sugar or rock sugar, plus more to taste (optional)

Pho Aroma

1 thumb-size knob ginger (cut lengthwise into ⅛-inch-thick, or 3 mm, slices)

3 shallots

6 coriander roots or 1 tbsp (15 ml) coriander seeds

1 cinnamon stick (optional)

2 star anise (optional)

It is common in Vietnam for home cooks to use both beef and chicken in the same pot of pho; however, many northern Vietnamese inist that *phở bò* (beef) and *phở gà* (chicken) are very different. In the beef version, we use more spices, such as star anise, black cardamom, and cinnamon, to counteract the strong beef smell. In the chicken version, we use more bulb and roots, such as shallots, ginger, and coriander, to bring an extra fresh and sweet aroma to the soup. This chicken version of pho takes a lot less time to cook than the beef recipe (page 44), but it still tastes exquisite.

INSTRUCTIONS

1. **To make the broth:** Sprinkle some salt over the chicken and rub on the skin to remove some of the poultry smell. Optional: Rinse the chicken well under cold running water and drain. Insert the scallion and ginger into its cavity—this will enhance the flavor of the meat as it cooks. Add the chicken, water, 1 tablespoon (15 ml) salt, 1 teaspoon chicken stock powder (if using), the onion, and 1 teaspoon sugar (if using) to a stockpot.

2. Bring to a boil, constantly skimming off the scum as soon as it rises to the top. When it boils, reduce the heat to low and cook, uncovered, until the chicken is tender. Occasionally skim off the scum. It might take 30 to 60 minutes depending on the kind of chicken you use. If the broth reduces, add hot water to compensate, making sure you always have the same amount as when you started.

3. **To make the pho aroma:** Heat the ginger, shallots, and coriander roots directly over an open flame on the stove until slightly charred on all sides. Peel the shallots, then rinse the shallots, ginger, and coriander under warm running water and scrape off the charred bits.

4. Toast the cinnamon stick (if using), star anise (if using), and coriander seeds (if using) in a pan over medium-low heat for 1 to 2 minutes, or until fragrant.

continued on page 48

Pho Bowl

3⅓ lb (1.5 kg) fresh or cooked pho
  noodles
5 kaffir lime leaves, rolled and
  sliced into fine threads
1 medium yellow onion, sliced very
  thin, soaked in ice water for
  15 minutes, and drained
3 to 5 scallions (green parts
  chopped; white parts kept
  whole, smashed, and blanched)
½ cup (30 g) chopped cilantro
3 sprigs sawtooth herb
3 sprigs Asian basil
1 lb (454 g) bean sprouts, blanched
1 lime, cut into wedges
3 bird's eye chili peppers, thinly
  sliced on the bias
Fish sauce (optional)
Sriracha (optional)
Hoisin (optional)
Pickled Garlic (page 164; optional)
Chili Jam (page 162; optional)

COOKING TIP

For a quicker weekday meal, use
store-bought chicken broth. You
can also freeze homemade broth
in ice-cube trays to have on hand
for busy days.

5. Place all of the pho aroma ingredients in a spice ball or large tea or
   spice bag(s), or wrap securely in a piece of cheesecloth. Add to the
   stockpot 30 minutes before serving, so the aroma stays fresh and
   tempting.

6. When you pierce the meat with a chopstick and see no pink water
   coming out, it is cooked. Remove the chicken from the stockpot
   and rinse well under cold running water to prevent the skin from
   darkening. Let cool, then debone. Slice the meat into bite-size pieces
   or shred roughly with your fingers. Return the bones to the stockpot
   and keep simmering for another 30 minutes. (Try not to leave any
   meat on the bones as it may make the soup cloudy.)

7. Season the broth to taste with salt, chicken stock powder (if using),
   and sugar (if using).

8. **To assemble the pho bowls:** Prepare the noodles following the
   package instructions, then rinse under cold water to stop the cooking
   process and remove the outside starch. Rinse again under hot water.
   This helps the noodles to dry faster and become fluffier, rather than
   sticking together and clumping.

9. Fill each serving bowl one-third full with noodles (about a handful
   of noodles). Top the noodles with chicken, lime leaf threads, onion
   slices, chopped scallions and cilantro, and blanched scallions.

10. Serve with a platter of the fresh herbs, blanched bean sprouts,
    lime wedges, and chili pepper slices, along with the fish sauce,
    hoisin sauce, sriracha, Pickled Garlic, and Chili Jam, if using these
    condiments.

PHO NOODLE SOUP WITH ROASTED DUCK

SKILL LEVEL: Advanced • **PREP TIME:** 40 minutes • **COOK TIME:** 2 hours 30 minutes • **YIELD:** 8 to 10 servings

INGREDIENTS

Duck

2 thumb-size knobs ginger, peeled, divided
1 tsp salt
1 whole duck (about 3⅓ lb, or 1.5 kg)
5 or 6 shallots, divided
1 tbsp (15 ml) five-spice powder
1 tbsp (15 ml) garlic powder
2 tbsp (36 g) oyster sauce
1 tsp cooking wine or *rượu Mai Quế Lộ* (rose cooking wine)
1 tsp salt
½ tsp black pepper
2 tsp sugar
1 tsp chicken stock powder
½ tsp annatto powder or paprika

Broth

16 cups (4 qt, or 4 L) water
4 to 5 lb (1.8 to 2.2 kg) chicken bones
1 medium yellow onion, halved, divided
1 tbsp (15 ml) salt, plus more to taste
1 tsp rock sugar, plus more to taste
10 dried sea worms (*sá sùng*), cut into 3-inch (7.5 cm) lengths, or 3 or 4 dried squids (optional)
3 star anise
1 cinnamon stick
Chicken stock powder, to taste

Duck Glaze

2 tbsp (30 ml) rice vinegar
1 tbsp (20 g) maltose or honey
½ tsp annatto powder or paprika

This recipe (*phở vịt quay*) comes out best if you can roast the duck in an oven with an auto-rotation function. The duck rotates constantly and browns very evenly. Maltose, or malt sugar, is popularly used in China for its sweetness and stickiness to roast duck—as it sticks to the skin and caramelizes, the roast duck takes on a lovely golden, shiny look. Annatto powder adds a bright orange-red color to the roast duck. If you can't find it, replace it with paprika.

INSTRUCTIONS

1. **To make the duck:** In a mortar and pestle, roughly crush 1 knob of ginger with the salt. Rub crushed ginger all over the duck, inside and out. Optional: Rinse the duck well under cold running water and drain.

2. To make the duck marinade, in a small bowl, combine the five-spice powder, garlic powder, oyster sauce, cooking wine, salt, black pepper, sugar, chicken stock powder, and annatto powder. Rub this mixture all over the duck, inside and out.

3. From the remaining ginger knob, cut 6 lengthwise slices, ⅛ inch (3 mm) thick. Insert 3 slices into the duck cavity, along with 2 or 3 peeled shallots. Set aside the remaining 3 ginger slices. Use a bamboo skewer to stitch and seal its cavity so that the ginger, shallots, and juices don't fall out while the duck is roasting. Let marinate in the refrigerator for 3 to 5 hours.

4. **To make the broth:** Fill a large stockpot with the water and add the chicken bones, an onion half, 1 tablespoons (15 ml) salt, and 1 teaspoon rock sugar. Bring to a boil, reduce the heat to low, and simmer, uncovered, for 1 to 2 hours. Occasionally skim off the scum. If the broth reduces, add hot water to compensate, making sure you always have the same amount as when you started.

5. **To make the duck glaze:** Combine the vinegar, maltose, and annatto powder, and brush all over the bird, starting with the first rotation and again at every rotation, for a shiny, crispy skin. Roast the duck in an oven preheated to 400°F (200°C) for 1 hour, rotating every 20 minutes (if you don't have the auto-rotation function).

Pho Bowl

3⅓ lb (1.5 kg) fresh or cooked pho noodles

3 to 5 scallions (green parts chopped; white parts kept whole, smashed, and blanched)

3 sprigs Asian basil

3 sprigs sawtooth herb

1 lb (454 g) bean sprouts, blanched

2 limes, cut into wedges

3 bird's eye chili peppers, thinly sliced on the bias

COOKING TIP

Use a whole chicken to make the broth if you can't find chicken bones. After boiling to make the broth, you can use the chicken meat to make something else. Sea worms (*sá sùng*) are extremely hard to find, especially overseas, but they are the secret for many pho restaurants in Hanoi. Dried sea worms can be replaced with dried squid. Make sure you grill or toss the squid in a hot pan to bring out the aroma. They add great depth of flavor to the broth. This dried seafood is a nice addition, but not a must.

6. In a pan over medium heat (without oil), toss the dried sea worms (if using), until fragrant and slightly golden. The dried sea worms will release lots of sand. Cut the sea worm tube open and rinse well a few times to get rid of all the sand. Insert into a filter bag and place in the broth 30 to 45 minutes before serving.

7. **To make the pho aroma:** Heat the remaining 3 shallots and remaining 3 slices ginger directly over an open flame on the stove until slightly charred on all sides. Peel the shallots, then rinse the shallots and ginger under warm running water and scrape off the charred bits.

8. Toast the cinnamon stick and star anise in a pan over medium-low heat for 1 to 2 minutes, or until fragrant.

9. Place all of the pho aroma ingredients in a spice ball or large tea or spice bag(s), or wrap securely in a piece of cheesecloth. Add to the stockpot 30 to 45 minutes before serving, so the aroma stays fresh and tempting.

10. Cut the remaining onion half into paper-thin slices, soak in ice water for 15 minutes, and drain.

11. After 1 hour of roasting the duck, increase the oven temperature to 500°F (250°C) and broil for another 10 minutes, rotating once, so the duck skin is evenly golden. Remove from the oven and let rest until cool. Gather the running juices from the cooked duck into a bowl to serve as a dipping sauce later. Before serving, debone and slice the duck meat into ⅛-inch-thick (3 mm) slices.

12. Season the broth to taste with salt, rock sugar, and/or chicken stock powder.

13. **To assemble the pho bowls:** Fill each serving bowl one-third full with noodles (about a handful of noodles). Top with duck meat and ladle the hot soup into the bowls. Top with chopped scallions, blanched scallions, and onion slices.

14. Serve with a platter of the fresh herbs, blanched bean sprouts, lime wedges, and chili pepper slices, along with the reserved duck roast juices as a dipping sauce or to be added to the pho bowl for more flavor.

PHO NOODLE SOUP WITH SEAFOOD

SKILL LEVEL: Intermediate • **PREP TIME:** 40 minutes • **COOK TIME:** 2 to 8 hours • **YIELD:** 8 to 10 servings

INGREDIENTS

Broth

6 lb (2.7 kg) beef bones (marrow and knuckle)
20 cups (5 qt, or 5 L) water
1 medium yellow onion, peeled
1 tbsp (15 ml) salt, plus more to taste
2 thumb-size pieces rock sugar, plus more to taste
1 onion, peeled
Chicken stock powder, to taste

Seafood

7 oz (200 g) whole shrimp
7 oz (200 g) cuttlefish, with skin, quill, eyes, interiors, and ink sacs removed
14 oz (400 g) shell-on clams or mussels, soaked in salted water to keep fresh
3½ oz (100 g) fish balls

Pho Aroma

3 shallots
4 slices ginger (cut lengthwise into ⅛-inch-thick, or 3 mm, slices)
1 cinnamon stick
2 black cardamom pods

Feel free to use other kinds of seafood in this soup (*phở hải sản*), such as mussels, scallops, salmon, or abalone.

INSTRUCTIONS

1. **To make the broth:** Place the beef bones in a large stockpot filled with enough water to cover them. Bring to a boil and cook for 5 to 10 minutes, until the impurities rise to the top. Drain the pot and rinse the bones well under running water.

2. Place the bones in a large stockpot with the water. (If you use the same pot as in step 1, make sure you clean it before putting the bones back. It is crucial for a clear broth.) Add the onion, 1 tablespoon (15 ml) salt, and 2 thumb-size pieces rock sugar to the stockpot. Bring to a boil, reduce the heat to low, and simmer, uncovered, for 2 to 8 hours—the longer the better. Occasionally skim off the scum. If the broth reduces, add hot water to compensate, making sure you always have the same amount as when you started. After 1 hour, remove the onion. Season the broth to taste with salt, rock sugar, and chicken stock powder.

3. **To prepare the seafood:** In a large pan, toast the shrimp (without oil) over high heat until they turn completely orange. Remove from the heat and let cool. Peel and devein. Reserve the shrimp shells for later use.

4. Slice the cuttlefish in half along the spine. On each half, with the tip of a very sharp knife, score parallel diagonal lines from end to end, about halfway into the flesh. Be careful not to cut all the way through. Repeat in the opposite direction to create a crisscross pattern. Then cut into 2-inch (5 cm) squares.

5. **To make the pho aroma:** Heat the shallots and ginger slices directly over an open flame on the stove until slightly charred on all sides. Peel the shallots, then rinse the shallots and ginger under warm running water and scrape off the charred bits.

6. Toast the cinnamon stick and cardamom pods in a pan over medium-low heat for 1 to 2 minutes, or until fragrant.

continued on page 54

Pho Bowl

3⅓ lb (1.5 kg) fresh or cooked pho
   noodles
1 onion, sliced very thin, soaked
   in ice water for 15 minutes, and
   drained
3 to 5 scallions (green parts
   chopped; white parts kept
   whole, smashed, and blanched)
3 sprigs Asian basil
3 sprigs sawtooth herb
1 lb (454 g) bean sprouts, blanched
   (optional)
1 lime, cut into wedges
3 bird's eye chili peppers, thinly
   sliced on the bias
Hoisin sauce (optional)
Sriracha (optional)

COOKING TIP

Scoring cuttlefish in a crisscross
pattern (*khứa vảy rồng*) helps
it curl up nicely when cooked.
Experiment with your knife by
keeping it at a 45-degree angle
while cutting. The end results will
differ, to your surprise.

7. Place all of the pho aroma ingredients and the reserved shrimp shells in a spice ball or large tea or spice bag(s), or wrap securely in a piece of cheesecloth. Add to the stockpot 30 to 45 minutes before serving, so the aroma stays fresh and tempting.

8. Extract the broth into a separate pot. If you are not serving it all at one go, only extract enough broth for the intended number of servings. Bring to a boil.

9. Add the clams to this pot and cook until they open. Remove with a slotted spoon and transfer to a plate.

10. Add the cuttlefish and cook for 2 minutes, or until it curls up and turns opaque. Remove with a slotted spoon and transfer to a plate. Repeat with the fish balls.

11. **To assemble the pho bowls:** Fill each serving bowl one-third full with noodles (about a handful of noodles). Arrange the clams, cuttlefish, shrimp, and fish balls on top of the noodles. Top with onion slices, blanched scallions, and chopped scallions. Ladle the hot broth over the noodles to fill the bowls.

12. Serve with a platter of the fresh herbs, blanched bean sprouts (if using), lime wedges, and chili pepper slices, along with the hoisin sauce and sriracha, if using these condiments.

VEGAN PHO NOODLE SOUP

SKILL LEVEL: Intermediate • **PREP TIME:** 20 minutes • **COOK TIME:** 1 hour • **YIELD:** 8 to 10 servings

INGREDIENTS

Broth

1 medium juicy red apple, peeled and cut into 2-inch (5 cm) cubes

1 medium Asian pear, peeled and cut into 2-inch (5 cm) cubes

2 medium carrots, peeled and sliced into 1-inch-thick (2.5 cm) rounds

1 kohlrabi, daikon radish, or chayote, peeled and cut into 2-inch (5 cm) cubes

1 leek, white part minced and green part cut into 3-inch (7.5 cm) lengths

1 medium yellow onion, peeled

16 cups (4 qt, or 4 L) water

1 tbsp (15 ml) salt, plus more to taste

1 thumb-size piece rock sugar, plus more to taste

Mushroom seasoning powder, to taste

Pho Aroma

2 shallots or 1 medium yellow onion

1 double-thumb-size knob ginger, sliced lengthwise into ⅛-inch-thick (3 mm) slices

3 star anise

2 cinnamon sticks

2 black cardamom pods

If you're a vegetarian or vegan who wants to enjoy Vietnamese cuisine, you only need to learn one word, *chay*, which translates to "vegetarian" in our language. Here's the vegetarian/vegan version of our national dish. Vary the fruits and vegetables for the broth to whatever is seasonal and available—you will need about four or five different types of vegetables and fruits.

INSTRUCTIONS

1. **To make the broth:** Add the apple, pear, carrots, kohlrabi, leek, onion, water, 1 tablespoon (15 ml) salt, and thumb-size piece rock sugar to a large stockpot. Bring to a boil, reduce the heat to low, and simmer, uncovered, for 30 minutes.

2. **To make the pho aroma:** Heat the shallots and ginger slices directly over an open flame on the stove until slightly charred on all sides. Peel the shallots, then rinse the shallots and ginger under warm running water and scrape off the charred bits.

3. Toast the star anise, cinnamon stick, and cardamom pods in a pan over medium-low heat for 1 to 2 minutes, or until fragrant.

4. Place all of the pho aroma ingredients in a spice ball or large tea or spice bag(s), or wrap securely in a piece of cheesecloth. Add to the stockpot 45 minutes before serving, so the aroma stays fresh and tempting.

5. **To make the toppings:** Arrange the tofu cubes on a paper towel and place another paper towel on top. Gently tap to remove the excess moisture in the tofu. Heat enough vegetable oil to cover the base of a large nonstick pan, then gently place the tofu cubes in the pan, leaving some space between them. Fry until golden brown on both sides. Remove from the pan and place on a paper towel–lined plate to drain the excess oil.

continued on page 56

Toppings

1 lb (454 g) tofu, cut into 1 x 2-inch
  (2.5 x 5 cm) pieces
Vegetable oil, for frying
7 oz (100 g) tofu skin or vegan beef
  slices, soaked in warm water for
  15 minutes and drained
Salt, to taste
Black pepper, to taste
1 tsp sugar, divided
1 tsp mushroom seasoning
  powder, divided, plus more to
  taste
1 tsp five-spice powder, divided
9 oz (250 g) mushrooms (such as
  straw, oyster, or shiitake)
10½ oz (300 g) vegan balls, thawed
  (optional)

Pho Bowl

3⅓ lb (1.5 kg) fresh or cooked pho
  noodles
3 sprigs sawtooth herb, chopped,
  plus 3 sprigs for serving
3 sprigs Asian basil
1 lb (454 g) bean sprouts, blanched
2 limes, cut into wedges
3 bird's eye chili peppers, thinly
  sliced on the bias
Sriracha (optional)
Hoisin sauce (optional)

SHOPPING TIP

Vegan balls are available in
the frozen section at Asian
food stores.

6. In a large bowl, combine the deep-fried tofu with the tofu skin, salt and black pepper to taste, and ½ teaspoon each of the sugar, mushroom seasoning powder, and five-spice powder.

7. Combine the mushrooms in a medium bowl with the remaining ½ teaspoon each sugar, mushroom seasoning powder, and five-spice powder.

8. Add the vegan balls (if using) to the stockpot. Season the soup to taste with salt and mushroom seasoning powder.

9. **To assemble the pho bowls:** Fill each serving bowl one-third full with noodles (about a handful of noodles). Add the toppings of your choice and garnish with chopped sawtooth herb. Ladle the hot soup over the noodles.

10. Serve with a platter of the fresh herbs, blanched bean sprouts, lime wedges, and chili pepper slices, along with sriracha or hoisin sauce, if using these condiments.

PHO NOODLE SOUP WITH BEEF STEW

SKILL LEVEL: Intermediate • **PREP TIME:** 30 minutes • **COOK TIME:** 1 hour 15 minutes • **YIELD:** 6 to 8 servings

INGREDIENTS

3 lb (1.4 kg) beef shank, tendon, and brisket (or shank or brisket), cut into 1 x 2-inch (2.5 x 5 cm) cubes

2 tsp sugar, plus more to taste

1 tsp salt, plus more to taste

1 tsp chicken stock powder, plus more to taste

½ tsp black pepper, plus more to taste

2 tsp *bò kho* or five-spice powder

1 tbsp (8 g) grated ginger

2 tbsp (30 ml) soy sauce

2 tbsp (20 g) minced garlic, divided

1 tbsp (15 ml) vegetable oil

4 stalks lemongrass, cut into 3-inch (7.5 cm) lengths and bruised

3 star anise

1 cinnamon stick

1½ cups (368 g) tomato sauce or 3 tbsp (48 g) tomato paste

1⅓ cups (315 ml) coconut water

6 cups (1.5 L) beef broth or water (see broth recipe in Simplified Pho Noodle Soup with Beef on page 44)

2 lb (907 g) carrots, peeled and cut into bite-size pieces

3 tbsp (45 ml) Annatto Oil (page 170; optional)

2 lb (907 g) fresh or cooked pho noodles

3 tablespoons (30 g) crispy fried shallot (*hành phi*; you can buy these at an Asian food store)

1 small yellow onion, sliced very thin, soaked in ice water for 15 minutes, and drained

3 sprigs sawtooth herb

3 sprigs Thai basil

In Vietnam, beef stew (*bò kho*) is commonly served as a hearty breakfast dish with freshly baked baguettes and a sunny-side-up egg. Some pho joints pour beef stew (sometimes diluted with beef broth) over pho noodles, and *voilà*, you have a new member of the pho family: *phở bò kho*. Coconut water is the secret to a naturally sweet broth.

INSTRUCTIONS

1. In a large bowl, combine the beef, 2 teaspoons sugar, 1 teaspoon salt, 1 teaspoon chicken stock powder, ½ teaspoon black pepper, *bò kho*, ginger, soy sauce, and 1 tablespoon (10 g) of the minced garlic. Mix well, cover, and let marinate in the refrigerator for at least 1 hour or overnight.

2. Heat the vegetable oil in a large wok or pan over medium-high heat. Add the remaining tablespoon (10 g) garlic, lemongrass, star anise, and cinnamon stick to the wok and cook and stir for 30 seconds to bring out the aroma. Add the marinated beef to the wok and stir-fry until no longer pink on the outside.

3. Add the tomato sauce, coconut water, and beef broth to the wok. Bring to a boil, cover, reduce the heat to low, and cook until the meat is tender, about 1 to 2 hours depending on the cut of beef you use. You can also use a pressure cooker, about 20 to 30 minutes.

4. When the beef is tender, add the carrots to the pan and cook until tender. Season to taste with salt, sugar, and chicken stock powder. Remove and discard the star anise and cinnamon stick. Add the Annatto Oil (if using).

5. Fill each serving bowl one-third full with noodles (about a handful of noodles). Ladle the beef stew over the noodles. Season with black pepper and garnish with fried shallot, onion slices, sawtooth herb, and Thai basil.

SHOPPING TIP

You can find *bò kho* powder (labeled as *Gia vị nấu bò kho*) at Asian food stores in the spice section. It's what gives this stew its unique flavor. If you can't find *bò kho*, five-spice powder is an acceptable substitute.

GIA LAI—STYLE DOUBLE-BOWL PHO

SKILL LEVEL: Intermediate • **PREP TIME:** 30 minutes • **COOK TIME:** 1 hour 30 minutes • **YIELD:** 6 servings

INGREDIENTS

Broth

2 lb (907 g) beef, pork, or chicken bones

12 cups (3 qt, or 3 L) water

1 medium yellow onion, peeled

2 thumb-size pieces rock sugar

2 tsp salt, plus more to taste

6-inch (15 cm) piece daikon, peeled and sliced into six 1-inch-thick (2.5 cm) rounds

Chicken stock powder, to taste

Toppings

7 oz (200 g) ground pork

Salt, to taste

Black pepper, to taste

2 oz (56 g) pork fatback, finely diced

3 tbsp (30 g) minced garlic

½ tsp sugar

3 shallots, thinly sliced

12 beef balls, thawed

This dish (*phở khô Gia Lai*) is a great noodle variation that combines pork and beef. It is unique to Gia Lai, a highland city in central Vietnam. Proudly named for that city, this dish is sometimes also called double-bowl pho (*phở 2 tô*) because it is served in two bowls, one for the noodles and one for the soup. Unlike the traditional soft and silky noodles for pho, the people of Gia Lai take pride in their regional noodles that are rice-based and thin yet chewy. These noodles are dry, but not easily breakable, so they are perfect for making a non-soup pho noodle dish. As it is very difficult to find them outside Gia Lai, you can use *hủ tiếu dai* noodles (see the Rice Noodle Directory, page 21) as a substitute.

INSTRUCTIONS

1. **To make the broth:** Place the bones in a large stockpot filled with enough water to cover them. Bring to a boil and cook the bones for 5 to 10 minutes, until the impurities rise to the top. Drain the pot and rinse the bones well under running water.

2. Place the bones in a large stockpot with the water. (If you use the same pot as in step 1, make sure you clean it before putting the bones back. It is crucial for a clear broth.) Add the onion, rock sugar, 2 teaspoons salt, and daikon rounds. Bring to a boil, reduce the heat to low, and simmer, uncovered, for 1 to 2 hours. Occasionally skim off the scum. If the broth reduces, add hot water to compensate, making sure you always have the same amount as when you started.

3. **To make the toppings:** In a medium bowl, season the ground pork with salt and pepper. Add a splash of water to the bowl and stir to separate the meat chunks.

4. Add the diced fatback to a medium pan over medium-high heat. Cook and stir to render the fat, about 5 minutes. When the fat pieces shrink and turn golden brown, remove them with a slotted spoon and transfer them (pork rinds) to a bowl. Set aside.

5. Add the garlic to the pork fat left in the pan and cook and stir over medium-low heat until golden brown. Remove the fried garlic from the pan with a slotted spoon, transfer to a bowl, and mix with the sugar, which helps keep the garlic crispy. Set aside.

continued on page 62

Pho Bowl

14 oz (400 g) dried Gia Lai–style noodles (*bánh phở khô Gia Lai*) or *hủ tiếu dai* noodles, soaked in room temperature water for 15 minutes and drained

3 cups (300 g) bean sprouts

2 tbsp (32 g) hoisin sauce, plus more for dipping

2 tbsp (30 ml) soy sauce

7 oz (200 g) beef sirloin or eye of round, very thinly sliced

5 scallions, chopped

3 sprigs cilantro, chopped

1 head soft-leaf lettuce

3 sprigs Asian basil

2 bird's eye chili peppers, thinly sliced on the bias

1 lime, cut into wedges

Sriracha, for dipping

SHOPPING TIP

You can buy beef balls frozen at Asian food stores. They are normally cooked before they're frozen, so you only need to warm them up in the broth.

6. Add the shallots to the pork fat left in the pan and cook and stir over medium-low heat until golden brown, about 1 minute. Remove the fried shallot with a slotted spoon and transfer to a bowl. Set aside.

7. Add the ground pork to the remaining fat in the pan and stir-fry over medium heat until it is cooked through. Use a spatula to break up any chunks. Turn off the heat.

8. Make a cross incision halfway through the beef balls, then add them to the broth (close to serving time) and cook for 5 minutes. Remove with a slotted spoon and transfer to an ice-water bath—this is to prevent discoloring and maintain a springy texture.

9. Season the broth to taste with salt and chicken stock powder.

10. **To assemble the pho bowls:** Add a handful of the Gia Lai–style noodles and some beansprouts to a noodle strainer. Submerge into a pot of boiling water for 30 seconds to blanch. Drain and toss with a teaspoon each of hoisin sauce and soy sauce until fully coated. Repeat for remaining servings.

11. Fill each serving bowl one-third full with noodles (about a handful of noodles). For each bowl, using a ladle, submerge a few slices of beef into the simmering broth to blanch for 5 seconds. Drain and place on top of the noodles, along with 2 tablespoons ground pork, 2 beef balls, and a teaspoon each of fried garlic, fried shallot, and pork rinds.

12. Fill separate serving bowls one-half to two-thirds full with the hot broth (maybe some bones, too), season with black pepper, and garnish with chopped scallions and cilantro.

13. Serve with a platter of the lettuce, Asian basil, chili pepper slices, and lime wedges, along with the hoisin sauce and sriracha for dipping.

THAI TOM YUM NOODLE SOUP

SKILL LEVEL: Easy • **PREP TIME:** 15 minutes • **COOK TIME:** 15 minutes • **YIELD:** 4 servings

INGREDIENTS

3-inch (7.5 cm) piece galangal, cut lengthwise into ¼-inch-thick (6 mm) slices

2 large cloves garlic

1 shallot

3 stalks lemongrass, cut on the bias into ¼-inch-thick (6 mm) slices

6 cups (1.5 L) water

5 kaffir lime leaves, torn with the stems still attached

1 tsp chicken stock powder

½ cup (50 g) straw mushrooms, halved

1 lb (454 g) prawns or shrimp, kept whole

3 bird's eye chili peppers, thinly sliced on the bias

1 tsp tom yum paste

½ medium yellow onion, thinly sliced lengthwise

3 tbsp (45 ml) fresh lime juice

3 tbsp (45 ml) fish sauce, plus more for dipping (optional)

1⅓ lb (600 g) fresh or cooked pho noodles

3 sprigs cilantro, chopped

Salt, to taste

Black pepper, to taste

1 lime, cut into wedges

Sriracha (optional)

Salt-Pepper-Lime Sauce (see Cooking Tip, below right); optional

This recipe is very quick and easy to put together. Basically, it is a Thai tom yum soup, but I've given it a little twist by applying this Vietnamese cooking technique: grill the root vegetables to bring out the aroma and give the soup more depth of flavor. Use whatever types of mushrooms you prefer.

INSTRUCTIONS

1. Heat the galangal, garlic, and shallot over an open flame on the stove until slightly charred on the outside. Peel the garlic and shallot, then rinse the garlic, shallot, and galangal under warm running water and scrape off the charred bits.

2. Add the charred ingredients, lemongrass, and water to a large stockpot. Bring to a boil, reduce the heat to medium-low, and simmer, uncovered, for 7 minutes to bring out the aroma.

3. Add the kaffir lime leaves and chicken stock powder to the stockpot. Increase the heat to high, add the mushrooms and prawns, and cook for 2 minutes, or until the prawns turn an orange-red color.

4. Add the chili pepper slices, tom yum paste, and onion slices to the stockpot, and cook for another minute over high heat. Turn off the heat.

5. Stir in the lime juice and 3 tablespoons (45 ml) fish sauce to the stockpot to maintain the fragrance and avoid making the broth bitter.

6. Fill each serving bowl one-third full with noodles (about a handful of noodles). Ladle the hot soup over the noodles. Top with chopped cilantro and season with salt and black pepper.

7. Serve with the lime wedges and Salt-Pepper-Lime Sauce, sriracha, and fish sauce, if using these condiments.

COOKING TIP

The best dipping sauce for seafood is this combination of salt, pepper, and lime (*muối tiêu chanh*): simply mix ½ teaspoon each of salt and black pepper, a pinch of sugar, and squeeze in a wedge of lime.

PHO NOODLE SOUP
WITH BEEF STEW IN RED WINE

SKILL LEVEL: Intermediate • **PREP TIME:** 30 minutes • **COOK TIME:** 1 hour (with beef broth prepared beforehand)
YIELD: 5 servings

INGREDIENTS

Beef

1 lb (454 g) beef flank or brisket, cut into 1 x 2-inch (2.5 x 5 cm) cubes
1 tbsp (10 g) minced or grated garlic
1 tbsp (6 g) minced or grated ginger
½ tsp five-spice powder
1 tsp sugar
1 tsp salt
1 tsp chicken stock powder
½ tsp black pepper
½ cup (120 ml) red wine, divided

Pho Aroma

2 shallots or 1 small yellow onion
1 thumb-size knob ginger, cut into ⅛-inch-thick (3 mm) slices
2 coriander roots
1 cinnamon stick
1 star anise
1 black cardamom pod

The red wine, bay leaves, and butter are what make this recipe (*phở bò sốt vang*) **more Western. Sautéing the onion in oil and adding the butter later helps maintain the butter smell and flavor. I use a pressure cooker to shorten the cooking time for the beef cubes. Feel free to use a normal pot, but it will take you double to triple the time. Using store-bought beef broth is another shortcut. If it is concentrated, dilute it with an equal amount of water.**

INSTRUCTIONS

1. **To make the beef:** In a large bowl, combine the beef cubes with the garlic, ginger, five-spice powder, sugar, salt, stock powder, black pepper, and ¼ cup (60 ml) of the red wine. Let marinate in the refrigerator for 2 hours.

2. **To make the pho aroma:** Heat the shallots, ginger slices, and coriander roots directly over an open flame on the stove until slightly charred on all sides. Peel the shallots, then rinse the shallots, ginger, and coriander under warm running water and scrape off the charred bits.

3. Toast the cinnamon stick, star anise, and cardamom pod in a pan over medium-low heat for 1 to 2 minutes, or until fragrant.

4. Place all of the pho aroma ingredients in a spice ball or large tea or spice bag(s), or wrap securely in a piece of cheesecloth.

5. **To make the broth:** Add the beef broth to a large stockpot and bring to a boil. Drop the spice bag into the pot, reduce the heat to low, and simmer, uncovered, for 30 minutes to infuse the broth with the pho aroma.

6. Heat the vegetable oil in a pressure cooker over medium-high heat. Add the onion and cook and stir until translucent. Add the marinated beef cubes and cook and stir until no longer pink on the outside.

Broth

8 cups (2 qt, or 2 L) beef broth (see broth recipe in Simplified Pho Noodle Soup with Beef on page 44)

2 tbsp (30 ml) vegetable oil

½ medium yellow onion, diced

1 tbsp (16 g) tomato paste

1 tbsp (15 g) unsalted butter

2 bay leaves

Salt, to taste

Rock sugar, to taste

3 tbsp (22 g) cornstarch

½ cup (120 ml) water

Pho Bowl

2 lb (907 g) fresh or cooked pho noodles

3 sprigs Asian basil, chopped

3 sprigs sawtooth herb, chopped

2 bird's eye chili peppers, thinly sliced on the bias

1 lime, cut into wedges

Salt-Pepper-Lime Sauce (see Cooking Tip on page 63)

SHOPPING TIP

Vietnamese five-spice powder is normally sold in a .35-ounce (10 g) packet and smells much stronger than Chinese five-spice powder, which is sold in small jars. If you use the Chinese type, use twice as much as called for in the recipe.

7. Add the tomato paste, butter, bay leaves, and remaining ¼ cup (60 ml) red wine to the pressure cooker. Pour in enough beef broth to barely cover the beef, about 1 cup (235 ml). Cover and cook for 15 minutes over low heat. Turn off the pressure cooker and let it cool down.

8. Remove the spice bag from the stockpot, then transfer the broth to the pressure cooker. Cover and bring to a boil.

9. Season the broth to taste with salt and rock sugar. (I use unsalted beef broth, so I add 1½ teaspoons salt and 2 teaspoons rock sugar.)

10. Dilute the cornstarch in the water, then pour into the pressure cooker to slightly thicken the broth.

11. **To assemble the pho bowls:** Fill each serving bowl one-third full with noodles (about a handful of noodles). Ladle the beef stew over the noodles. Garnish with Asian basil and sawtooth herb. Serve with chili pepper slices, lime wedges, and Salt-Pepper-Lime Sauce for dipping the beef.

PHO NOODLE DISHES

Các món phở khác

PHO PIZZA

SKILL LEVEL: Intermediate • **PREP TIME:** 30 minutes • **COOK TIME:** 30 minutes • **YIELD:** 2 servings

INGREDIENTS

10½ oz (300 g) beef tenderloin, thinly sliced against the grain

Salt, to taste

Black pepper, to taste

6 tbsp (90 ml) vegetable oil, divided

2 tbsp (20 g) minced garlic, divided

1 tbsp (18 g) oyster sauce, divided

1 tbsp (15 ml) tapioca starch or cornstarch, divided

10½ oz (300 g) fresh or cooked pho noodles, separated, divided

1 small carrot, sliced into thin rounds and halved

1 small red bell pepper, cut into 1-inch (2.5 cm) squares

1 small yellow bell pepper, cut into 1-inch (2.5 cm) squares

½ medium yellow onion, peeled and cut into wedges

7 oz (200 g) Chinese celery, cut into 2-inch (5 cm) lengths

7 oz (200 g) bok choy, leaves separated and rined

½ tsp chicken stock powder, plus more to taste

1 tbsp (15 ml) dark soy sauce, plus more to taste

¼ cup (60 ml) water

1 tablespoon (10 g) crispy fried shallot (*hành phi*; you can buy these at an Asian food store)

1 bird's eye chili pepper, thinly sliced on the bias

In Vietnam, you will find this dish (*phở áp chảo*) served at night at Chinese noodle stores. Besides beef, you can also use seafood (such as shrimp and squid), or if you are feeling adventurous, pig organs.

INSTRUCTIONS

1. Season the beef with salt, black pepper, 1 tablespoon (15 ml) of the vegetable oil, 1 tablespoon (10 g) of the garlic, ½ tablespoon (9 g) of the oyster sauce, and ½ tablespoon (7.5 ml) of the tapioca starch. Give it a good mix and let it marinate for about 15 minutes.

2. To make the crispy noodles, heat 3 tablespoons (45 ml) of the vegetable oil in an 8-inch (20 cm) pan over medium heat. When the oil is hot, add half of the pho noodles. Use a spatula to press the noodles, so they stick together and form into a "cake." Fry both sides until golden brown. Remove from the pan and place on a paper towel–lined plate to drain the excess oil. Repeat with the remaining pho noodles. Set aside.

3. Heat 1 tablespoon (15 ml) of the vegetable oil in a large wok or pan over medium-high heat. Add the remaining 1 tablespoon (10 g) garlic and cook and stir until fragrant. Toss in the beef and stir-fry over high heat until no longer pink on the outside. Transfer the beef back to the bowl it was marinating in.

4. Keeping the heat on high, add the remaining 1 tablespoon (15 ml) vegetable oil to the wok along with the carrot. Stir-fry for 1 minute, then add the bell peppers and onion. Stir-fry for 1 to 2 minutes, then add the Chinese celery and bok choy.

5. Reduce the heat to very low and season the vegetables with the ½ teaspoon chicken stock powder, 1 tablespoon (15 ml) dark soy sauce, and remaining ½ tablespoon (9 g) oyster sauce. Mix well.

6. Increase the heat to medium. Combine the remaining ½ tablespoon (7.5 ml) tapioca starch with the water and add to the stir-fry. Return the beef to the wok and mix well. Cook for 1 to 2 more minutes, until the sauce turns translucent and is slightly thickened. Taste and adjust the flavor with soy sauce and/or stock powder. Turn off the heat.

7. Cut the crispy pho bases into triangle slices and place on a serving platter. Top with the stir-fry. Sprinkle some black pepper, fried shallot, and chili pepper slices on top. Serve hot while the noodle base is still crispy.

CRISPY PHO PILLOWS WITH SALMON

SKILL LEVEL: Intermediate • **PREP TIME:** 30 minutes • **COOK TIME:** 35 minutes • **YIELD:** 2 servings

INGREDIENTS

Pho Pillows

7 oz (200 g) rice noodle sheets (see Rice Noodle Batter instructions for Fresh Pho Rolls, page 81)
Vegetable oil, for frying

Sauce

1 tbsp (15 g) tomato sauce
1 tbsp (18 g) oyster sauce
1 tsp chicken stock powder
½ tsp sugar
½ tbsp (9 g) chili sauce
½ tsp sesame oil
½ cup (120 ml) water

Stir-Fry

2 salmon fillets (7 oz, or 200 g, each)
Salt, to taste
Black pepper, to taste
1 tbsp (15 ml) vegetable oil
1 tsp minced garlic
¾ cup (70 g) straw mushrooms or mushrooms of choice, halved
⅓ cup (40 g) julienned carrot
⅓ cup (40 g) julienned bell pepper
⅓ cup (40 g) julienned celery
⅓ cup (40 g) julienned onion
2 scallions, cut into 2-inch (5 cm) lengths

The people of Hanoi are known as "pho addicts," and their appreciation of the pho noodle goes beyond the soup bowl. This dish (*phở chiên phồng*) is just one of their fun creations. In Hanoi, it is normally served with beef and stir-fried greens, such as bok choy or spinach. I learned this variation that uses salmon from Chef Phuoc Hung on *Món ngon mỗi ngày*, a daily cooking show on Vietnamese television.

INSTRUCTIONS

1. **To make the pho pillows:** Place 3 rice noodle sheets on top of one another and cut into 1-inch (2.5 cm) squares.

2. Place a small saucepan over medium heat. Fill with vegetable oil to a depth of 2-inches (5 cm). Heat until the oil reaches 360°F (180°C), or test the temperature with a chopstick inserted into the oil: when bubbles appear around the chopstick, the oil is ready for deep-frying.

3. Gently drop the pho squares into the saucepan, leaving some space between them at first so they do not stick together. After 30 to 60 seconds, the surface should no longer be sticky, so you can push the squares closer together and add more to the pan. Fry over medium heat until puffy (like a pillow) and golden brown, about 3 minutes. Remove from the pan with a slotted spoon and place on a paper towel–lined plate to drain the excess oil. You will need to fry in batches.

4. **To make the sauce:** In a small bowl, combine the tomato sauce, oyster sauce, chicken stock powder, sugar, chili sauce, water, and sesame oil. Stir well to dissolve. Set aside.

continued on page 72

5. **To make the stir-fry:** Season the salmon fillets on both sides with salt and pepper. Heat the vegetable oil in a large pan over medium-high heat until hot. Add the salmon and sear both sides—sear the skin side until golden and crispy. Remove from the pan and let rest on a plate.

6. Add the garlic to the same pan and stir and cook over medium-high heat until fragrant. Add the mushrooms and stir and cook for 30 seconds. Add the carrot, followed by the bell pepper and celery. Stir-fry for 3 minutes, then mix in the sauce.

7. Add the onion and stir-fry for another minute, then turn off the heat. Mix in the scallions.

8. Divide the stir-fry between the two serving plates. Arrange the crispy pho pillows around the stir-fry so they don't turn soggy. Place the seared salmon on top of the stir-fry.

STIR-FRIED PHO WITH SEAFOOD

SKILL LEVEL: Intermediate • **PREP TIME:** 40 minutes • **COOK TIME:** 25 minutes • **YIELD:** 2 servings

INGREDIENTS

Seafood Stir-Fry

3½ oz (100 g) cuttlefish, with skin, quill, eyes, interiors, and ink sacs removed

3½ oz (100 g) shrimp, peeled and deveined

1 tsp salt, plus more to taste

Black pepper, to taste

1 tbsp (6 g) minced scallion, white part only, divided

1 tbsp (10 g) minced garlic, divided

1 tbsp (6 g) minced ginger, divided

1 tsp cooking wine

1 tsp cornstarch

7 tbsp (105 ml) vegetable oil, divided

½ large carrot, thinly sliced

3½ oz (100 g) snow peas, strings removed

3½ oz (100 g) baby corn

7 oz (200 g) baby bok choy, rinsed and quartered

7 oz (200 g) dried pho noodles, soaked in water for 30 minutes and drained

3½ oz (100 g) fish cake, thinly sliced into bite-size pieces

2 oz (56 g) mushrooms (such as shiitake or straw)

For this recipe (*phở xào hải sản*)**, use vegetables you prefer. Picking vegetables of various colors makes a pretty dish. For greens, you can use bok choy, garlic chives, snow peas, or broccoli; for red/orange, use bell peppers and carrots; for yellow, use baby corn or cauliflower. Adding vegetable oil to the blanching water gives the vegetables a shiny, fresh look.**

INSTRUCTIONS

1. **To make the seafood stir-fry:** Slice the cuttlefish in half along the spine. On each half, with the tip of a very sharp knife, score parallel diagonal lines from end to end, about halfway into the flesh. Be careful not to cut all the way through. Repeat in the opposite direction to create a crisscross pattern. Cut the fish into 2-inch (5 cm) squares.

2. In separate bowls, soak the cuttlefish and shrimp in salted water for 5 minutes, then drain.

3. In separate bowls, season the cuttlefish and shrimp with salt and black pepper, along with 1 teaspoon each of the scallion, garlic, ginger, cooking wine, and cornstarch. Mix well and set aside.

4. Bring a medium saucepan of water to a boil. Add the 1 teaspoon salt and 1 tablespoon (15 ml) of the vegetable oil. Blanch the carrots for 2 minutes, then remove; blanch the snow peas for 2 minutes, then remove; and blanch the baby corn for 2 minutes, then remove. For the bok choy, dip the stems in the boiling water first and hold for 30 seconds, then drop in the whole leaves and blanch for another 30 seconds.

5. Heat 2 tablespoons (30 ml) of the vegetable oil in a large wok or pan over medium-high heat. Add the remaining scallion, garlic, and ginger, and cook and stir until fragrant, about 15 seconds.

Sauce
1 tbsp (18 g) oyster sauce
1 tsp sesame oil
2 tbsp (30 ml) soy sauce
2 tbsp (30 g) tomato sauce
½ cup (120 ml) water

Garnish and Seasonings
3 sprigs cilantro, chopped
½ tsp white pepper
Few drops sesame oil

6. Add the shrimp to the wok and sear both sides for 1 to 2 minutes. Transfer to a clean plate and set aside.

7. Add 2 tablespoons (30 ml) of the vegetable oil and the cuttlefish to the wok. Cook and stir until the cuttlefish curls and turns opaque, about 2 minutes. Transfer to a clean plate and set aside.

8. **To make the sauce:** Combine the oyster sauce, sesame oil, soy sauce, tomato sauce, and water in a medium bowl.

9. Add the remaining 2 tablespoons (30 ml) vegetable oil to the same wok the seafood was cooked in. Add the blanched vegetables and the sauce, and cook and stir for 2 minutes.

10. Add the soaked noodles to the wok and stir-fry for 3 minutes. Return the shrimp and cuttlefish to the wok, tossing well and cooking for another 1 to 2 minutes.

11. Transfer the stir-fry to a serving platter and top with cilantro, white pepper, and sesame oil.

COOKING TIP

Stir-frying noodles can be frustrating because the noodles can get mushy or clumpy. To prevent this from happening, soak them in water for 15 minutes before cooking. The heat of the vegetables and seafood in the wok then cooks them in just a few minutes. Try not to crowd the wok when stir-frying, as stirring too much breaks the noodles. Ideally, stir-fry one serving at a time so that the heat reaches each ingredient evenly. If you multiply the recipe, stir-fry in batches. I use a 12-inch (30 cm) wok, which works well for this recipe for two.

PHO OMELET

SKILL LEVEL: Easy • **PREP TIME:** 5 minutes • **COOK TIME:** 10 minutes • **YIELD:** 1 serving

INGREDIENTS

1 egg

1 tsp fish sauce

¼ tsp black pepper

Vegetable oil, for frying

5½ oz (150 g) fresh or cooked pho noodles, separated

1 scallion, chopped

Sweet chili sauce or sriracha, to taste, for serving

Pickled Carrots and Daikon (page 165), to taste, for serving

After finding some leftover pho noodles in my refrigerator one day, I created this omelet (*phở chiên trứng*), which has the flavor of one of my favorite snacks from southern China: fried rice flour cakes with eggs (*bột chiên*). To balance out the fried flavor, I added some Pickled Carrots and Daikon (page 165). *Voilà!* A brilliant combination, if I do say so myself!

INSTRUCTIONS

1. Crack the egg in a small bowl and add the fish sauce and black pepper. Beat well.

2. Fill a 9-inch (22 cm) pan with just enough vegetable oil to cover the bottom and heat to 375°F (180°C). Keep the heat at medium and spread the pho noodles over the pan. Fry until slightly golden brown throughout.

3. Pour in the beaten egg and cook until it solidifies. Add the scallion to the pan halfway through cooking.

4. Serve with a squirt of hot sauce and the Pickled Carrots and Daikon.

COOKING TIP

When frying the noodles, pour just enough vegetable oil to cover the bottom of the pan—too little oil is not enough to crisp up the noodles and too much oil makes them limp.

CRISPY PHO WITH BEEF AND CHOY SUM STIR-FRY

SKILL LEVEL: Intermediate • **PREP TIME:** 30 minutes • **COOK TIME:** 25 minutes • **YIELD:** 2 servings

INGREDIENTS

7 oz (200 g) beef tenderloin, thinly sliced against the grain

Salt, to taste

Black pepper, to taste

3 tbsp (45 ml) vegetable oil, divided, plus more for frying

1 tbsp (10 g) minced garlic, divided

1 tsp plus 1 tbsp (18 g) oyster sauce, divided

1 tsp stock powder (optional)

2 tsp tapioca starch or cornstarch, divided, plus ⅓ cup (40 g) to coat the noodles

7 oz (200 g) fresh or cooked pho noodles

⅓ cup (80 ml) water

7 oz (200 g) choy sum, cut into 2-inch (5 cm) lengths and rinsed

2 egg yolks, lightly beaten

½ medium yellow onion, peeled and cut into wedges

1 tbsp (15 ml) soy sauce

2 tbsp (20 g) crispy fried shallot (*hành phi*; you can buy these at an Asian food store), for garnish

1 bird's eye chili pepper, thinly sliced on the bias, for garnish

As customers are constantly seeking out innovative pho dishes, this dish (*phở chiên giòn xào bò*) is one of the newer creations of pho restaurants in Vietnam. Choy sum (*rau cải ngọt*) is a leafy green vegetable commonly used in Chinese stir-fries. You can substitute the choy sum with bok choy or spinach.

INTRUCTIONS

1. In a large bowl, combine the beef with salt, black pepper, 1 tablespoon (15 ml) of the vegetable oil, 1 teaspoon of the minced garlic, 1 teaspoon of the oyster sauce, stock powder (if using), and 1 teaspoon of the tapioca starch. Give it a good mix and let it marinate for 15 minutes.

2. To make the crispy pho noodles, in a tray, separate the noodles with your hands. Mix the noodles with the beaten egg yolks, then fluff to coat with ⅓ cup (40 g) of the tapioca starch. Shake off the excess starch.

3. Place an 8-inch (20 cm) pan over medium heat. Fill with vegetable oil to a depth of 2 inches (5 cm). Heat until the oil reaches 360°F (180°C), or test the temperature with a chopstick inserted into the oil: when bubbles appear around the chopstick, the oil is ready for deep-frying.

4. Add the pho noodles to the saucepan one handful at a time and deep-fry over medium heat until golden and crispy. The noodles might stick to each other but you should still see the individual strings. Remove from the pan with a slotted spoon and place on a paper towel–lined plate to drain the excess oil. Divide the noodles between two serving plates.

5. In a small bowl, dissolve the remaining 1 teaspoon tapioca starch and the remaining 1 tablespoon (18 g) oyster sauce with the water to form a slurry. Set aside.

6. Heat 1 tablespoon (15 ml) of the vegetable oil in a large wok or pan over high heat. Add the remaining 2 teaspoons garlic and cook and stir until fragrant. Add the choy sum and stir-fry until wilted, 3 to 4 minutes. Add the onion and stir-fry for 1 minute. Stir in the soy sauce, then pour the stir-fried greens on top of the crispy noodles.

7. Keeping the heat on high, add the remaining 1 tablespoon (15 ml) vegetable oil to the wok and stir-fry the beef until no longer pink on the outside.

8. Pour the oyster-sauce slurry over the beef in the wok. Simmer for 1 minute until thickened, then pour the beef and sauce over the stir-fried greens.

9. Serve immediately with a sprinkle of black pepper and garnished with the fried shallot and chili pepper slices.

FRESH PHO ROLLS

SKILL LEVEL: Intermediate • **PREP TIME:** 40 minutes • **COOK TIME:** 1 hour • **YIELD:** 10 to 15 rolls

INGREDIENTS

Rice Noodle Batter
1 cup (158 g) rice flour
1 cup (120 g) tapioca starch or
    cornstarch
2 cups (475 ml) water
½ tsp salt
2 tsp vegetable oil

Beef Stir-Fry
12½ oz (354 g) beef (such as
    rumpsteak), thinly sliced againt
    the grain
2 tsp minced garlic, divided
1 tsp minced ginger
½ tsp salt
1 tsp chickcn stock powder
    (optional)
½ tsp black pepper
1 tbsp (15 ml) vegetable oil, plus
    more for stir-frying
1 medium yellow onion, thinly
    sliced lengthwise (optional)
Fresh greens and herbs such as
    lettuce, mint, perilla, and cilantro

Serving
Fish Sauce Dressing (page 167)

COOKING TIP

For a tidy roll, try not to stuff it
with too much filling—a little bit
goes a long way.

Here's a creative way to serve pho in the form of fresh spring rolls (*phở cuốn*), which originated in Hanoi. Traditionally, the rice noodle sheets are made in a special kind of steamer found in Vietnamese markets; it cooks the batter into a perfect silky sheet on a piece of cloth stretched over a pot of boiling water. But this steamer is bulky and hard to find outside of Vietnam, so I have included a method that you can use with more common kitchen equipment.

INSTRUCTIONS

1. **To make the rice noodle batter:** Combine the rice flour, tapioca starch, water, salt, and vegetable oil in a large bowl. Let rest for 1 hour.

2. **To make the beef stir-fry:** Season the beef with 1 teaspoon of the garlic, ginger, salt, chicken stock powder (if using), black pepper, and 1 tablespoon (15 ml) vegetable oil. Mix well and let sit for 15 minutes.

3. Heat some vegetable oil in a large wok or pan over high heat. Add the remaining 1 teaspoon garlic and cook and stir until fragrant. Add the beef and stir-fry over high heat until no longer pink on the outside. Do not overcook. Add the onion (if using) and cook until slightly translucent, about 1 minute. Remove from the heat and set aside.

4. Place an 8-inch (20 cm) round or a 4 x 8-inch (10 x 20 cm) rectangular plate on the steaming rack in a steamer. Steam the plate for 1 to 2 minutes, until hot. Stir up the rice noodle batter and ladle over just enough batter to cover the base of the plate. Steam for 4 to 5 minutes, until set and quite translucent.

5. Run a spatula around the edges of the rice noodle sheet and carefully peel it off the plate. Repeat with the remaining batter. You can stack the rice sheets on top of each other when done.

6. **To assemble the pho rolls:** Place a rice sheet on a flat surface and top with some fresh greens, herbs, and beef. Lift the bottom end of the rice sheet and wrap it up over the filling, securing the roll closed gently but tightly.

7. Serve immediately with some Fish Sauce Dressing.

PHO SALAD WITH BEEF AND TAMARIND SAUCE

SKILL LEVEL: Easy • **PREP TIME:** 30 minutes • **COOK TIME:** 10 minutes • **YIELD:** 4 to 6 servings

INGREDIENTS

1 lb (454 g) beef (such as rumpsteak), thinly sliced against the grain

Salt, to taste

Black pepper, to taste

2 tbsp (20 g) minced garlic, divided

1 tbsp (10 g) minced shallot, divided

1 tsp chicken stock powder

1 tbsp (18 g) oyster sauce

1 tbsp (15 ml) vegetable oil, plus more for stir-frying

1 tsp tapioca starch or cornstarch

5 oz (150 g) tamarind pulp

2 cups (475 ml) water

1 to 2 tbsp (15 to 30 g) butter

½ cup (100 g) sugar or palm sugar

½ cup (120 ml) fish sauce

2 lb (907 g) fresh or cooked pho noodles, tossed with some vegetable oil

1 lb (454 g) bean sprouts, blanched

3 sprigs Asian basil

3 sprigs Vietnamese balm

3 sprigs mint

¼ cup (36 g) crushed roasted peanuts, for garnish

3 bird's eye chili peppers, thinly sliced on the bias, for garnish

This quick and easy summer salad (*phở trộn sốt me*) **is one that you're sure to enjoy on those extremely hot days when you don't really feel like eating anything, let alone cooking.**

INSTRUCTIONS

1. In a large bowl, combine the beef with salt, black pepper, 1 tablespoon (10 g) of the garlic, ½ tablespoon (5 g) of the shallot, chicken stock powder, oyster sauce, 1 tablespoon (15 ml) vegetable oil, and tapioca starch. Mix well, cover, and let marinate in the refrigerator for 30 minutes.

2. Add the tamarind pulp and water to a small saucepan. Bring to a boil and cook for 5 to 10 minutes, until the pulp breaks up. (Use a spoon to help break it up.) Strain the pulp through a sieve to get the tamarind sauce. Set aside.

3. Add the butter to a medium pan over medium heat. Add the remaining 1 tablespoon (10 g) garlic and the remaining ½ tablespoon (5 g) shallot to the pan, and cook and stir until fragrant. Add the tamarind sauce, sugar, and fish sauce to the pan. Taste and adjust as needed to achieve a balance of flavor. Turn off the heat and let cool.

4. Heat some vegetable oil in a large wok or pan over high heat. Add the beef and stir-fry until the beef is no longer pink on the outside, 3 to 4 minutes. Don't overcook.

5. To assemble the pho bowls, fill each serving bowl one-third full with noodles (about a handful of noodles) and drizzle the sweet-and-sour tamarind sauce over the top. Give it a good mix, then add blanched bean sprouts and herbs. Top with the stir-fried beef and garnish with a sprinkle of crushed roasted peanuts and some chili pepper slices.

COOKING TIP

Marinating beef with vegetable oil and tapioca starch is a great way to keep it moist and tender. Always add the oil and starch after the other seasonings so they coat each beef slice, locking in flavor and juices.

VEGAN PHO SALAD WITH MUSHROOMS

SKILL LEVEL: Easy • **PREP TIME:** 15 minutes • **COOK TIME:** 10 minutes • **YIELD:** 4 servings

INGREDIENTS

3 tbsp (45 ml) vegetable oil, divided
2 shallots, thinly sliced
1 tbsp (10 g) minced garlic, divided
¼ cup (61 g) tomato sauce
¼ cup (60 ml) soy sauce
2 tsp sugar
¼ tsp red chili flakes (optional)
1⅔ lb (750 g) fresh or cooked pho noodles
7 oz (200 g) various mushrooms, roots trimmed and separated (if using enoki) or sliced
Salt, to taste
Black pepper, to taste
2 scallions, finely chopped
2 tbsp (16 g) roasted sesame seeds
1 medium tomato, sliced

Here's a simple, super-healthy recipe (*phở trộn nấm*) you can put together in a jiffy. Use a variety of mushrooms, such as oyster, beech, enoki, shiitake, and straw mushrooms, or any other mushrooms that you prefer. It would be perfect to offer this dish in the fall after a mushroom harvest!

INSTRUCTIONS

1. Heat 2 tablespoons (30 ml) of the vegetable oil in a large wok or pan over medium heat. Add the shallots and fry until golden brown. Remove the fried shallots with a slotted spoon and transfer to a small bowl. Set aside.

2. Add ½ tablespoon (5 g) of the minced garlic to the the wok and cook and stir until fragrant.

3. Add the tomato sauce, soy sauce, and sugar to the wok. Mix well and simmer for 30 seconds, until smooth. Add the chili flakes to the pan (if using). Turn off the heat. Transfer one-third of the sauce to a small bowl and set aside.

4. Separate the noodles with your fingers and toss with the remaining sauce in the wok.

5. In a separate large pan, add the remaining 1 tablespoon (15 ml) vegetable oil and the remaining ½ tablespoon (5 g) garlic, and cook and stir until fragrant.

6. Add the mushrooms to the pan and stir-fry for 1 to 2 minutes. Depending on the kinds of mushrooms you use, add the ones that take longer to cook first (like king oyster or beech mushrooms), followed by quick-cooking ones (like enoki and straw mushrooms). Season to taste with salt and black pepper. Remove the pan from the heat.

7. Divide the noodles among the serving plates. Top with the sautéed mushrooms and garnish with chopped scallions, roasted sesame seeds, and fried shallots.

8. Serve with the tomato slices and reserved sauce for a dipping sauce.

PHO SALAD WITH CHAR SIU

SKILL LEVEL: Easy • **PREP TIME:** 40 minutes • **COOK TIME:** 40 minutes • **YIELD:** 6 servings

INGREDIENTS

1.76 oz (50 g) roast red pork seasoning mix

2 tbsp (20 g) minced garlic

1 tbsp (6 g) grated ginger

1 tbsp (15 ml) salt

1 tbsp (15 ml) soy sauce

1 tbsp (15 ml) sesame oil

1 tbsp (18 g) oyster sauce

2 tbsp (40 g) honey

3 tbsp (45 ml) vegetable oil, divided

1 tbsp (15 ml) cooking wine

3 tbsp (45 ml) plus ½ cup (120 ml) water, divided

1 lb (454 g) pork shoulder, cut into long bars, about 1 x 2 inches (2 x 4 cm) thick

2 lb (907 g) fresh or cooked pho noodles

1 head leaf lettuce, torn into small pieces

2 cups (200 g) bean sprouts, blanched

3 sprigs Asian basil

3 bird's eye chili peppers, thinly sliced on the bias, for garnish

½ cup (80 g) crispy fried shallot (*hành phi*; you can buy these at an Asian food store), for garnish

This recipe (*phở xíu*) tastes simply divine, and the secret is roast red pork seasoning mix (*char siu* powder). Choose a pork shoulder that still has some fat on it, so the meat will be juicy. This marinade sounds like a lot for 1 pound (454 g) of meat, but since you'll make the sauce with it, it comes out just right in the end.

INSTRUCTIONS

1. Combine the roast red pork seasoning mix, garlic, ginger, salt, soy sauce, sesame oil, oyster sauce, honey, 1 tablespoon (15 ml) of the vegetable oil, wine, and 3 tablespoons (45 ml) of the water in a large bowl, and stir to dissolve. Add the pork to the bowl and submerge in the marinade. Cover with plastic wrap. Let marinate in the refrigerator for at least 2 hours or overnight.

2. Preheat the oven to 500°F (250°C). Place the marinated pork on a baking tray lined with aluminum foil, reserving the marinade. Broil for 15 minutes, then flip and cook for another 20 minutes at 400°F (200°C).

3. Remove the meat from the oven and let cool on a rack for 20 minutes, then cut into thin slices.

4. Heat the remaining 2 tablespoons (30 ml) vegetable oil in a large wok or pan over medium heat.

5. Add the reserved marinade to a small saucepan and dilute with the remaining ½ cup (120 ml) water to make a sauce. Bring to a boil. Remove from the heat.

6. To assemble the pho bowl, fill each serving bowl one-third full with noodles (about a handful of noodles). Add 2 tablespoons (30 ml) of the sauce to each bowl and mix to coat the noodles.

7. Place some lettuce, blanched bean sprouts, and Asian basil around the sides of the bowls, and arrange 5 or 6 slices of *char siu* on top.

8. Garnish with chili pepper slices and the fried shallot, and mix well before serving.

VERMICELLI NOODLE SOUPS

Các món bún nước

HUE-STYLE SPICY BEEF VERMICELLI NOODLE SOUP

SKILL LEVEL: Intermediate • **PREP TIME:** 60 minutes • **COOK TIME:** 1 hour 30 minutes • **YIELD:** 10 servings

INGREDIENTS

Broth

2¼ lb (1 kg) beef bones
2¼ lb (1 kg) pork trotters (pig's front feet)
20 cups (5 qt, or 5 L) water
2¼ lb (1 kg) beef shank
6 stalks lemongrass, bruised
1 medium yellow onion, peeled
1 tbsp (15 ml) salt, plus more to taste
1 thumb-size piece rock sugar
2 tbsp (30 g) fermented tiny shrimp paste (*mắm ruốc*)
3 cups (700 ml) cold water, divided
Fish sauce, to taste
Chicken or pork stock powder, to taste (optional)

Sa Tế

3 tbsp (45 ml) vegetable oil
1 tbsp (8 g) minced lemongrass
1 tbsp (10 g) minced garlic
1 tbsp (10 g) minced shallot
1 tbsp (15 ml) chili powder or red chili flakes
1 tbsp (15 ml) water
2 tbsp (30 ml) fish sauce
2 tbsp (30 ml) sugar

This dish (*bún bò Huế*) originated in Huế, once the capital of Vietnam, but it is loved by all Vietnamese for its bold flavors. Though simmering the bones for two to three hours makes for a heartier broth, I normally don't have that much time on a regular day. Sometimes I use a pressure cooker to speed things up. By multitasking, I can manage to cook this dish within an hour and a half.

INSTRUCTIONS

1. **To make the broth:** Place the beef bones and the pork trotters in a large stockpot. Fill with enough water to cover them. Bring to a boil and cook for 5 to 10 minutes, until the impurities rise to the top. Drain the pot and rinse the bones well under running water to wash off the impurities.

2. Place the bones and pork trotters in a large stockpot and fill with the water. (If you use the same pot as in step 1, make sure you clean it before putting the bones and trotters back. It is crucial for a clear broth.) Add the beef shank to the stockpot.

3. Tie up the lemongrass stalks and add to the stockpot. (To tie up lemongrass, you can use either the outer layer of one stalk as a "string" or kitchen twine.) Add the onion, 1 tablespoon (15 ml) salt, and rock sugar to the pot. Bring to a boil, reduce the heat to medium-low, and simmer, uncovered, for 60 to 90 minutes, depending on the size of the meat. Occasionally skim off the scum. If the broth reduces, add hot water to compensate, making sure you always have the same amount as when you started.

4. When the beef shank and pork trotters are cooked, remove the meat and soak it in a bowl of cold water for 5 minutes to prevent it from turning dark. Drain and let cool, then thinly slice into bite-size pieces.

5. Meanwhile, continue simmering the bones for 1 to 2 more hours. You can add a few more lemongrass stalks in the last hour for a more fragrant broth.

continued on page 90

Vermicelli Bowl

3⅓ lb (1.5 kg) fresh or cooked thick rice vermicelli noodles (normally labeled as *bún bò Huế*)

14 oz (400 g) boiled blood cubes (*huyết*; optional)

7 oz (200 g) Vietnamese shrimp patties (*chả Huế*; optional)

7 oz (200 g) Vietnamese ham (*chả lụa*; optional)

1 cup (100 g) chopped scallion

1 cup (60 g) chopped cilantro

1 medium yellow onion, sliced very thin, soaked in ice water for 15 minutes, and drained

Fresh greens and herbs such as mint or Vietnamese mint, shredded banana blossom, and shredded lettuce or shredded cabbage

7 oz (200 g) bean sprouts

6. **To make the sa tế:** Heat the vegetable oil in a small pan over medium heat and cook and stir the minced lemongrass, garlic, and shallot until fragrant and slightly golden. Remove from the heat.

7. In a small bowl, combine the chili powder, water, fish sauce, and sugar, then add to the pan from step 6. Stir well, place the pan back on the stove, and simmer over low heat for 2 minutes, until smooth. Add half of this *sa tế* to the stockpot and reserve the rest in a small bowl for serving.

8. Dissolve the fermented shrimp paste in 1 cup (235 ml) of the cold water. Let sit for 10 minutes to allow the dregs to settle.

9. Add the remaining 2 cups (475 ml) cold water and the shrimp paste liquid (discard the dregs at the bottom) to a small saucepan. Bring to a boil, then remove from the heat and let sit for 15 minutes, undisturbed, to allow the dregs to settle again. Extract the clear broth on top and add to the simmering stockpot anytime during the last hour. Discard the dregs. Adjust the flavor of the broth to your taste with salt, fish sauce, and chicken stock powder.

10. **To assemble the vermicelli bowls:** Fill each serving bowl one-third full with noodles (about a handful of noodles). Top with the sliced beef and pork. Add the boiled blood cubes, Vietnamese shrimp patties, and Vietnamese ham (*chả lụa*), if using. Ladle the broth over the noodles and top with the scallion, cilantro, and onion slices.

11. Serve with the reserved *sa tế* and a platter of herbs, fresh greens, and bean sprouts.

SHOPPING TIP

Mắm is the key to Vietnamese cuisine. It is the general term that refers to various kinds of fermented seafood. Besides the very popular fish sauce (*nước mắm*), we also have squid sauce (*mắm mực*), anchovy sauce (*mắm nêm*), fermented shrimp sauce (*mắm tôm*), fermented small shrimp sauce (*mắm tép*), and fermented tiny shrimp paste (*mắm ruốc*). This recipe calls for *mắm ruốc*, which is made from *ruốc* (tiny shrimp); it's unique to central Vietnam. It is dense with a dark brown or muddy red color. Strong tasting, a small amount is enough to deepen the flavor of a large pot of broth. You can buy this in small glass jars at Asian food stores. Look for the label "*Mắm ruốc Huế*," as this is obviously best to use in *bún bò Huế*!

DUCK VERMICELLI NOODLE SOUP WITH BAMBOO SHOOTS

SKILL LEVEL: Intermediate • **PREP TIME:** 40 minutes • **COOK TIME:** 1 hour • **YIELD:** 4 to 6 servings

INGREDIENTS

Broth
2 thumb-size knobs ginger, peeled, divided

1 tsp plus 1 tbsp (20 ml) salt, divided, plus more to taste

1 tbsp (15 ml) alcohol (such as vodka)

1 whole duck (about 3⅓ lb, or 1.5 kg)

2 or 3 shallots, peeled

½ medium yellow onion, peeled

Bamboo Shoots
14 oz (400 g) bamboo shoots, torn into strips

¼ cup (60 ml) vegetable oil

5 shallots, thinly sliced

1 tbsp (10 g) minced garlic

2 tsp chicken stock powder

1 tsp sugar

½ tsp salt

This soup (*bún măng vịt*) is one of the most classic Vietnamese poultry noodle soup dishes. You can use chicken instead of duck (then it is called *bún măng gà*), but the version with duck is more flavorful. Ginger-Flavored Dipping Fish Sauce is a must-have if you are cooking duck, and this dish would be lacking without it.

INSTRUCTIONS

1. **To make the broth:** In a mortar and pestle, roughly crush a thumb-size piece of ginger with 1 teaspoon of the salt. Add the alcohol to the mortar and combine. Rub this mixture all over the duck, inside and out. Optional: Rinse the duck well under cold running water.

2. With the remaining knob of ginger, cut 3 slices lengthwise, ⅛-inch-thick (3 mm). Insert the 3 slices and 2 or 3 shallots into the duck's cavity.

3. Place the duck in a large stockpot and fill with enough water to cover it. Add the onion and the remaining 1 tablespoon (15 ml) salt to the stockpot. Bring to a boil, skim off the scum, reduce the heat to low, and simmer for 30 to 45 minutes, depending on the size of the duck. Occasionally skim off the scum. If the broth reduces, add hot water to compensate, making sure you always have the same amount as when you started.

4. **To make the bamboo shoots:** Place the bamboo shoots in a small saucepan. Fill with enough water to cover them. Bring to a boil and cook for 3 to 5 minutes to remove the toxins inside of them. Drain and rinse under running water. Squeeze out the excess water from the bamboo shoots. Set aside.

continued on page 92

Vermicelli Bowl

2 lb (907 g) fresh or cooked rice
  vermicelli noodles

¼ head green cabbage, shredded
  very finely

4 to 6 scallions (white parts kept
  whole, smashed, and blanched)

¼ head green cabbage, shredded
  very finely

½ cup (30 g) chopped Vietnamese
  mint

¼ cup (15 g) chopped sawtooth
  herb

½ cup (30 g) chopped cilantro

1 yellow onion, sliced very thin,
  soaked in ice water for
  15 minutes, and drained

1 lime, cut into wedges

3 bird's eye chili peppers, thinly
  sliced on the bias

Ginger-Flavored Dipping Fish
  Sauce (page 167)

SHOPPING TIP

You'll find a wide variety of
bamboo shoots at Asian food
stores. Fresh shoots are packaged
in plastic bags, whole or shredded,
or you can buy them dried. Dried
bamboo shoots will add great
flavor to a soup, but what a
challenge to prepare! You need to
soak them in water you've washed
rice in for three nights, changing
the water each time, and then
boil them three times uncovered
until they're tender enough to eat.
Luckily, some stores sell prepared
dried bamboo shoots (*măng khô
nấu sẵn*) in a package, to spare
you the trouble. Using a variety
of bamboo shoots will add more
texture to your noodle soup bowl,
making it more fun to eat.

5. Heat the vegetable oil in a large wok or pan over medium heat. Add
   the shallots and fry until golden brown. Remove the fried shallots
   with a slotted spoon and transfer to a small bowl. Set aside.

6. Add the garlic to the pan and cook and stir over medium heat until
   fragrant. Add the bamboo shoots to the pan and stir-fry for a couple
   of minutes. Reduce the heat to low and add the chicken stock
   powder, sugar, and salt. Mix well, increase the heat to medium-high,
   and stir-fry for 3 to 5 minutes. Remove from the heat.

7. To test the duck, pierce the leg with a chopstick or fork and when the
   water coming out runs clear, it's cooked through. Remove the duck
   from the stockpot and rinse under cold running water to prevent
   darkening. Drain and let cool completely.

8. Remove the onion from the stockpot and discard. Add the stir-fried
   bamboo shoots to the stockpot and cook for 15 minutes. Season
   the broth with salt, chicken stock powder, and sugar to your desired
   taste.

9. Cut the duck in half lengthwise along the spine. Detach the legs and
   drumsticks, and remove the bones near the breast. Slice the breast
   into bite-size pieces. Place the duck meat on top of a serving platter
   of the shredded cabbage.

10. **To assemble the vermicelli bowls:** Fill each serving bowl one-third
    full with noodles (about a handful of noodles). Arrange a few slices
    of duck meat on top. Add some shredded cabbage and blanched
    scallions. Ladle the hot soup with the bamboo shoots over the
    noodles and top with the chopped herbs, sliced onion, and fried
    shallots.

11. Serve with the lime wedges and chili pepper slices, along with the
    Ginger-Flavored Dipping Fish Sauce.

DA NANG-STYLE FISH CAKE AND VEGETABLE VERMICELLI NOODLE SOUP

SKILL LEVEL: Intermediate • **PREP TIME:** 30 minutes • **COOK TIME:** 1 hour • **YIELD:** 6 to 8 servings

INGREDIENTS

Fish Cake

7 oz (200 g) clown or featherback knifefish paste *(cá thát lát nạo)*

7 oz (200 g) catfish paste

3½ oz (100 g) pork fatback, diced

2 scallions (white parts only), minced

2 tbsp (30 ml) all-purpose flour

1 tsp chicken stock powder

2 tsp salt

1 tsp black pepper

1 tbsp (15 ml) sugar

1 egg

3 tbsp (45 ml) vegetable oil, plus more for greasing

Broth

16 cups (4 qt, or 4 L) chicken, fish, or pork broth

1 lb (454 g) pumpkin, unpeeled and cut into 2-inch (5 cm) cubes

14 oz (400 g) bamboo shoots, shredded (see Shopping Tip on page 92)

3 medium tomatoes, cut into wedges

10½ oz (300 g) pineapple, peeled, eyes and core removed, and sliced

10½ oz (300 g) green cabbage, cut into 2-inch (5 cm) pieces

¼ cup (60 ml) Annatto Oil (page 170)

Sugar, to taste

Salt, to taste

Chicken stock powder, to taste

Fish sauce, to taste

This soup (*bún chả cá*) is one of the signature dishes of Da Nang. A variety of vegetables go into this broth, which is very tasty and healthy. It is best to use fish, chicken, or pork broth to prepare the soup, but using plain water is fine, too. The sweetness of the soup comes mostly from the vegetables. Not peeling the pumpkin keeps the cubes in shape even after they're cooked in the soup for a long time. We don't want the cubes to break up and make the soup cloudy.

INSTRUCTIONS

1. **To make the fish cake:** In a large bowl, combine both fish pastes, along with the pork fatback, scallions, flour, chicken stock powder, salt, black pepper, sugar, and egg. Mix well.

2. Grease a mortar and pestle with some vegetable oil. Transfer the fish-paste mixture to the mortar and pound by hand until it is a consistent texture—this helps to create the chewy texture of the fish cake. If you have a stand mixer, use the flat paddle attachment to mix the paste for 5 to 10 minutes.

3. To shape the fish cake, place a large piece of plastic wrap on a 7-inch (18 cm) round plate and transfer a portion of the paste onto it. Flatten and shape the paste into a 1-inch-thick (2.5 cm) disk. Alternatively, you can shape the fish paste with your hands into 1-inch (2.5 cm) fish balls or 2-inch (5 cm) patties. Repeat with the remaining paste.

4. Heat the 3 tablespoons (45 ml) vegetable oil in a small pan over medium-high heat. Fry the fish cakes on both sides until golden brown. Alternatively, you can steam them for 20 minutes to make steamed fish cakes. Cut them into bite-size pieces.

Vermicelli Bowl

3⅓ lb (1.5 kg) fresh or cooked rice vermicelli noodles

½ cup (50 g) chopped scallion

1 cup (60 g) chopped cilantro

1 head leaf lettuce, leaves torn into small pieces or shredded

3 sprigs each of herbs such as mint, perilla, or Asian basil, stems removed and roughly chopped

2 cups (200 g) bean sprouts, blanched

1 lime, cut into wedges

Fermented tiny shrimp paste (*mắm ruốc*)

5. **To make the broth:** Bring the chicken broth to a boil in a large stockpot. Add the pumpkin, reduce the heat to medium, and cook for 20 minutes.

6. Add the bamboo shoots, tomatoes, pineapple, and cabbage. Keep cooking over medium heat for another 15 minutes.

7. Add the fish-cake pieces and Annatto Oil to the stockpot, then season to taste with sugar, salt, chicken stock powder, and fish sauce.

8. **To assemble the vermicelli bowls:** Fill each serving bowl one-third full with noodles (about a handful of noodles). Ladle the broth, fish-cake pieces, and vegetables over the noodles. Top with the scallion and cilantro.

9. Serve with a platter of the lettuce, herbs, blanched bean sprouts, and lime wedges, along with the fermented shrimp paste.

SHOPPING TIP

Clown or featherback knifefish paste (*cá thát lát nạo*) is available frozen at Asian food stores. It gives the fish cake a chewy, springy texture. Catfish paste is also available frozen, or you can grind mackerel, catfish, or tilapia fillets into a paste. Experiment with different kinds of fish or combine them to get the texture and flavor you prefer.

CHICKEN CURRY WITH VERMICELLI NOODLES

SKILL LEVEL: Intermediate • **PREP TIME:** 30 minutes • **COOK TIME:** 1 hour • **YIELD:** 6 servings

INGREDIENTS

Curry

2¼ lb (1 kg) bone-in chicken, cut into bite-size pieces

1 tsp salt, plus more to taste

1 tsp sugar

1 tsp chicken stock powder, plus more to taste

½ tsp black pepper

1 tbsp (15 ml) curry powder

1 lb (454 g) potatoes, peeled, cut into 1-inch (2.5 cm) cubes, soaked in slightly salted water, and drained

1 lb (454 g) sweet potatoes, peeled, cut into 1-inch (2.5 cm) cubes, soaked in slightly salted water, and drained

1 lb (454 g) taro, peeled, cut into 1-inch (2.5 cm) cubes, soaked in slightly salted water, and drained

¼ cup (60 ml) plus 1 tbsp (15 ml) vegetable oil, divided

1 tbsp (10 g) minced garlic

1 tbsp (10 g) minced shallot

1 tbsp (6 g) minced ginger

2 stalks lemongrass, bruised

1 cup (235 ml) coconut milk

6 cups (1.5 L) coconut water

Vermicelli Bowl

2 lb (907 g) fresh or cooked rice vermicelli noodles

3 sprigs Asian basil

1 cup (100 g) bean sprouts

2 bird's eye chili peppers, thinly sliced on the bias

¼ cup (36 g) crushed roasted peanuts

Lemongrass, different types of potatoes, and coconut milk are what distinguish Vietnamese chicken curry (*bún cà ri gà*) from other types of curries. I find that the natural sweetness of the coconut water makes the curry heartier, but you can substitute chicken broth or plain water. Feel free to use boneless chicken; just remember to reduce the cooking time.

INSTRUCTIONS

1. **To make the curry:** In a large bowl, combine the chicken with the 1 teaspoon salt, black pepper, sugar, 1 teaspoon chicken stock powder, and curry powder. Let marinate in the refrigerator for at least 30 minutes or overnight.

2. Remove any excess water from the cubed potatoes, sweet potatoes, and taro using a paper towel. Heat ¼ cup (60 ml) of the vegetable oil in a large pan over high heat. Add the potatoes, sweet potatoes, and taro to the pan and fry until the outsides are golden brown and crispy—this is to keep them in shape and prevent a mushy texture in the curry. Remove from the pan and place on a rack or a paper towel–lined tray to drain excess oil.

3. Heat the remaining 1 tablespoon (15 ml) vegetable oil in a large wok or pan over medium-high heat. Add the garlic, shallot, and ginger to the pan, and cook and stir until fragrant, about 1 minute.

4. Add the marinated chicken to the wok and stir well. Cook over high heat to sear the chicken on all sides. Transfer to a stockpot.

5. Add the lemongrass, coconut milk, and coconut water to the stockpot. Bring to a boil and skim off the scum. Add the fried potatoes, sweet potatoes, and taro. Season to taste with salt and chicken stock powder. Reduce the heat to medium-low and simmer for 30 to 45 minutes, or until the potatoes and chicken are fork-tender.

6. **To assemble the vermicelli bowls:** Fill each serving bowl one-third full with noodles (about a handful of noodles). Ladle the chicken curry over the noodles. Garnish with a few Asian basil leaves, bean sprouts, chili pepper slices, and crushed roasted peanuts.

PORK AND MUSHROOM VERMICELLI NOODLE SOUP

SKILL LEVEL: Intermediate • **PREP TIME:** 30 minutes • **COOK TIME:** 1 hour 30 minutes • **YIELD:** 6 to 8 servings

INGREDIENTS

Broth

2¼ lb (1 kg) pork spare ribs
1 tbsp (15 ml) white vinegar
16 cups (4 qt, or 4 L) water
1 medium yellow onion, peeled and halved
1 tsp rock sugar, plus more to taste
1 tbsp (15 ml) salt, plus more to taste
5 shallots
½ oz (15 g) dried shiitake mushrooms, stems removed, rinsed, soaked in warm water for 15 minutes, drained, and excess water squeezed out
2 tbsp (30 g) fermented shrimp sauce (*mắm tôm*), divided
½ cup (120 ml) cold water
Chicken stock powder, to taste

Pork and Mushroom Balls

½ oz (15 g) dried woodear mushrooms, soaked in hot water for 15 minutes, drained, excess water squeezed out, and minced
1 tbsp (10 g) minced shallot
1 tbsp (15 ml) fish sauce, plus more to taste
7 oz (200 g) pork paste (*chả quết*)
½ tsp black pepper, plus more to taste

This soup (*bún mọc*) originated in northern Vietnam. In the process of migrating to the South, the dish was adapted: more *chả* was added and the flavor of the soup became bolder and somewhat sweeter. *Chả* is the Vietnamese word for processed meat products in the form of ham, sausages, and pork balls.

INSTRUCTIONS

1. **To make the broth:** Place the spare ribs in a large stockpot filled with enough water to cover them. Add the vinegar to the stockpot, bring to a boil, and cook for 5 minutes, until the impurities rise to the top. Drain the pot and rinse the ribs well under running water to wash off the impurities.

2. Place the ribs in a large stockpot and fill with the water. (If you use the same pot as in step 1, make sure you clean it before putting the ribs back. It is crucial for a clear broth.) Add the onion, 1 teaspoon rock sugar, and 1 tablespoon (15 ml) salt to the stockpot. Bring to a boil and skim off the scum. Reduce the heat to medium-low heat and simmer, uncovered, for 1 to 2 hours. Occasionally skim off the scum. If the broth reduces, add hot water to compensate, making sure you always have the same amount as when you started.

3. Heat the shallots directly over an open flame on the stove until slightly charred on all sides. Peel the shallots, then rinse under warm running water and scrape off the charred bits. Add to the stockpot at the beginning of the last hour of simmering to enhance the aroma. Add the shiitake mushrooms.

4. **To make the pork and mushroom balls:** In a medium bowl, combine the woodear mushrooms with the minced shallot and 1 tablespoon (15 ml) fish sauce. Add the pork paste and ½ teaspoon black pepper to the bowl, and combine. Cover the bowl with plastic wrap and refrigerate for 30 minutes, for a crunchier texture.

Vegetable Side Platter

3 elephant ear stems, peeled and
　　cut into ¼-inch-thick (6 mm)
　　slices on the bias

2 tsp salt

2 oz (57 g) water spinach stems,
　　split into fine strings

2 oz (57 g) banana blossom, thinly
　　sliced

Vermicelli Bowl

2 lb (907 g) fresh or cooked rice
　　vermicelli noodles

3½ oz (100 g) cinnamon ham
　　(*chả quế*), cut into bite-size pieces

3½ oz (100 g) Vietnamese ham
　　(*chả lụa*), cut into ¼-inch-thick
　　(6 mm) slices

3½ oz (100 g) pork sausage in
　　banana leaves (*chả Huế*), cut into
　　bite-size pieces

1 cup (60 g) chopped cilantro

¼ cup (40 g) crispy fried shallot
　　(*hành phi*; you can buy these at
　　an Asian food store)

3 bird's eye chili peppers, thinly
　　sliced

SHOPPING TIP

You can buy *chả* frozen at Asian
food stores. It's easier to look
for the Vietnamese word on the
packaging.

5. Form the chilled pork-and-mushroom paste into 1-inch (2.5 cm) balls
   and drop them into the stockpot. Cook until they float to the surface.
   Remove with a slotted spoon and transfer to an ice bath for
   15 minutes to prevent darkening.

6. In a small bowl, combine the fermented shrimp sauce with the cold
   water. Stir until dissolved and let sit for 15 minutes to allow the dregs
   to settle. Extract the clear liquid on top and add to the stockpot
   to intensify the flavor of the broth. Discard the dregs settled at the
   bottom. Bring the broth to a boil over medium heat.

7. Reduce the heat to simmer and season the broth to taste with salt
   and chicken stock powder.

8. **To prepare the vegetable side platter:** Combine the elephant ear
   stems with the salt and let sit for 15 minutes. Squeeze out the excess
   water from the stems and rinse a few times with warm water. Wear
   gloves for this step, as the elephant ear stems may cause itchiness.

9. Bring a large saucepan of water to a boil. Blanch the split water
   spinach, sliced banana blossom, and elephant ear stems separately
   for 30 seconds per batch. Drain and place on a serving platter.

10. **To assemble the vermicelli bowls:** Fill each serving bowl one-third
    full with noodles (about a handful of noodles). Arrange the variety of
    ham, sausage, and pork and mushroom balls on top, then ladle the
    hot soup over. Top with the fried shallot and chili pepper slices.

11. Serve with the vegetable side platter.

HANOI COMBO VERMICELLI NOODLE SOUP

SKILL LEVEL: Intermediate • **PREP TIME:** 30 minutes • **COOK TIME:** 45 minutes • **YIELD:** 6 servings

INGREDIENTS

Broth

1 tbsp (15 ml) salt, plus more to taste

1 whole chicken (about 2½ lb, or 1.2 kg)

1 scallion

4 slices ginger (cut lengthwise into ⅛-inch-thick, or 3 mm, slices), divided

16 cups (4 qt, or 4 L) water

1 medium yellow onion, peeled

3 tbsp (35 g) dried shrimp, soaked in hot water for 15 minutes and drained

8 dried shiitake mushrooms, stems removed, soaked in hot water for 15 minutes, drained, and excess water squeezed out

Fish sauce, to taste

Chicken stock powder, to taste

Egg Topping

4 eggs

Salt, to taste

Black pepper, to taste

¼ cup (60 ml) fish sauce

1 tsp vegetable oil, for greasing

This soup (*bún thang*) is one of the most popular and sophisticated noodle soup dishes in Hanoi cuisine. Traditionally, it is prepared on the fourth day of our Lunar New Year (*Tết*), as it incorporates leftovers from the holiday feasts, including Vietnamese ham, chicken, and mushrooms. There's one theory that it's called *bún thang* because when assembling the dish, you take a bit of every topping, similar to when you are assembling an herbal medicine prescription (*thang thuốc*). There's another theory that says *thang* comes from the Chinese and Korean word for "soup." So *bún thang* would be soup made with *bún*. An elegant dish, the toppings are sliced into very fine strips, not julienned. They should be as fine as papaya shredded with a vegetable shredder.

INSTRUCTIONS

1. **To make the broth:** Sprinkle some salt over the chicken and rub it into the skin to remove the poultry smell. Rinse the chicken well under cold running water. Insert the scallion and 2 slices of the ginger into its cavity—this will enhance the flavor of the meat as it cooks.

2. To a large stockpot, add the chicken, water, 1 tablespoon (15 ml) salt, the remaining 2 slices ginger, and the onion. Bring to a boil and skim off the scum as soon as it rises to the top. Add the shrimp and shiitake mushrooms to the stockpot, reduce the heat to medium-low, and simmer, uncovered, until the chicken is tender. It might take 30 to 60 minutes depending on the kind of chicken you use. Occasionally skim off the scum. If the broth reduces, add hot water to compensate, making sure you always have the same amount as when you started.

3. **To make the egg topping:** In a medium bowl, add the eggs and lightly season with salt and black pepper. Add the fish sauce, then beat well.

continued on page 102

Vermicelli Bowl

2 lb (907 g) fresh or cooked rice vermicelli noodles

7 oz (200 g) sweet-and-sour preserved radish, shredded (you can buy this at an Asian food store)

7 oz (200 g) Vietnamese ham (*chả lụa*), shredded

3 salted eggs, hard-boiled, peeled, and halved (you can buy these at an Asian food store; optional)

½ cup (30 g) chopped Vietnamese mint leaves

1 cup (100 g) chopped scallion

1 lime, cut into wedges

2 tbsp (30 g) fermented shrimp sauce (*mắm tôm*)

3 drops *Lethocerus indicus* extract (*cà cuống*; optional)

SHOPPING TIP

Lethocerus indicus is a giant water bug native to Southeast Asia. In northern Vietnam, a tiny drop of its essence added to a bowl of dipping sauce (served with steamed rice rolls known as *banh cuốn*) or to a bowl of *bún thang* is believed to add great flavor and uniqueness to the dish.

4. Grease an 8-inch (20 cm) nonstick pan with the vegetable oil, then use a paper towel to wipe it off. Heat the pan over medium heat until it is nice and hot. Pour the egg mixture into the pan and tilt it in a circular motion to coat the bottom. Quickly pour the egg mixture back into the bowl; you will get a very thin egg sheet sticking to the pan. Remove the sheet and let it cool on a plate or cutting board. Repeat this step until you finish the egg mixture. (You only need to grease the pan for the first sheet.)

5. To test the chicken, poke the thigh with a chopstick or fork and when the water coming out runs clear, it is cooked through. Remove from the stockpot and rinse well under cold running water to prevent the skin from darkening. Let cool, then debone and thinly shred the meat by hand.

6. Remove the shiitake mushrooms from the stockpot with a slotted spoon, thinly slice, and set aside.

7. Season the broth to taste with salt, fish sauce, and chicken stock powder, and simmer for 5 more minutes after you remove the chicken.

8. Roll up the egg sheets and cut into very thin strips.

9. Arrange the shredded chicken, sliced mushrooms, and egg sheet strips side by side on a serving platter.

10. **To assemble the vermicelli bowls:** Fill each of the serving bowls halfway with noodles. Top with shredded chicken, preserved radish, shredded ham, sliced shiitake, egg strips, and ½ salted egg (if using). Ladle the hot soup over the noodles. Top with the chopped mint and scallion.

11. Serve with the lime wedges, fermented shrimp sauce (*mắm tôm*), and *Lethocerus indicus* extract (if using).

CRAB AND TOFU VERMICELLI NOODLE SOUP

SKILL LEVEL: Advanced • **PREP TIME:** 1 hour 30 minutes • **COOK TIME:** 45 minutes • **YIELD:** 6 to 8 servings

INGREDIENTS

2 lb (907 g) rice field crabs

1½ tsp salt, divided

6 cups (1.5 L) water, divided

4 tbsp (60 g) fermented shrimp sauce (*mắm tôm*), divided

3 tbsp (45 ml) vegetable oil

3 shallots, thinly sliced

½ tsp annatto powder or paprika

3 medium tomatoes, cut into wedges

1 tsp chicken stock powder, plus more to taste

1 tbsp (15 ml) fish sauce, plus more to taste

4 cups (1 qt, or 1 L) pork broth or water (see pork broth recipe in Pork and Mushroom Vermicelli Noodle Soup on page 98)

3 tbsp (35 g) dried shrimp, soaked in warm water for 15 minutes and drained

⅔ cup (160 ml) cold water

1 cup (225 g) fried tofu puffs (you can buy these or fry them yourself)

2 lb (907 g) fresh or cooked rice vermicelli noodles

½ cup (50 g) chopped scallion

½ cup (30 g) chopped cilantro

1 head leaf or iceberg lettuce, shredded

3 sprigs perilla or Vietnamese balm, stems removed and

If you've tried this soup (*bún riêu cua*) outside of Vietnam, it was probably not authentic; the real *bún riêu cua* has to be made from rice field crabs, which are mostly only available in Vietnam and a few other countries that grow rice. They are smaller than three inches (7.5 cm) and live in rice fields to feed off young rice. As they are so small, there is not much meat on them to eat, but the Vietnamese invented this method of cooking the crabs to get the most out of them. Though it's best to buy and cook rice field crabs when they're still alive, some Asian food stores do offer them frozen whole or in a black crab paste.

INSTRUCTIONS

1. Toss the crabs with 1 teaspoon of the salt and rinse a few times to get rid of the mud. Wear gloves to remove the claws and carapaces. Use a toothpick to pick out the orange stuff (*gạch cua*) inside the body and gather it in a small bowl. Be patient, as this process may take a while.

2. Place the crab bodies in a food processor and pulse to grind to a fine paste. Alternatively, pound in a mortar and pestle.

3. Transfer the crab paste to a large bowl and add 3 cups (70 ml) of the water. Mix well. Let the mixture run through a mesh strainer to extract the liquid. Repeat with the remaining 3 cups (700 ml) water. Discard the shell.

4. To make the broth, pour the extracted crab liquid into a medium saucepan. Add the remaining ½ teaspoon salt and bring to a boil. Reduce the heat to low and add 1 teaspoon of the fermented shrimp sauce. Stop stirring and cook for 3 minutes. The protein will form in this time and float to the surface. That is the real *riêu cua*! Turn off the heat.

5. Use a slotted spoon to transfer the *riêu cua* to a bowl and set aside in a cold place or refrigerate to chill and set.

6. Heat the vegetable oil in a large pan over medium heat. Add the shallots and fry until golden brown. Remove half of the fried shallots

If you can't find the live or frozen field crabs, substitute cans of minced crab in spices, commonly available at most Asian food stores. Here is the recipe for the easy and express version of *riêu cua*:

1 can (5.6 oz, or 160 g) minced crab in spices (*gia vị nấu bún riêu*)
3 eggs
10½ oz (300 g) ground pork
1 tbsp (15 ml) fish sauce
½ tsp black pepper

Combine all ingredients in a large bowl and mix well. Pour into a pot of boiling pork broth (about 10 cups, or 2.5 L) and cook until it floats to the surface. The rest of the steps are the same as the original recipe (see from step 5).

with a slotted spoon and transfer to a small bowl. Set aside.

7. Add the reserved orange stuff (*gạch cua*) to the shallots and oil in the pan, and cook and stir over medium heat for a couple of minutes. Add the annatto powder, tomato wedges, 1 teaspoon chicken stock powder, and 1 tablespoon (15 ml) fish sauce, and stir-fry for 3 minutes, or until the tomatoes are soft but not broken.

8. To the crab broth, add the pork broth, stir-fried tomatoes, and dried shrimp, and cook over medium-high heat.

9. In a small bowl, combine 2 tablespoons (30 g) of the fermented shrimp sauce with the cold water. Stir until dissolved and let sit for 15 minutes to allow the dregs to settle. Extract the clear juice on top and add to the broth to intensify the flavor. Discard the dregs settled at the bottom. Bring the broth to a boil over medium heat, then reduce the heat to a simmer.

10. Add the fried tofu puffs to the broth and season to taste with fish sauce and chicken stock powder. Turn off the heat.

11. To assemble the vermicelli bowls, fill each serving bowl one-third full with noodles (about a handful of noodles). Scoop a few spoonfuls of the *riêu cua* on top. Ladle the hot soup with tofu puffs and tomato over the noodles. Top with chopped scallion, chopped cilantro, and crispy fried shallot.

12. Serve with a platter of the lettuce, herbs, and lime wedges, along with the remaining fermented shrimp sauce.

VERMICELLI NOODLE DISHES

Các món bún khác

VERMICELLI NOODLE DISH ACCOMPANIMENTS

INGREDIENTS

1 head leaf or iceberg lettuce, leaves torn into small pieces or shredded

3 sprigs each of herbs such as mint, perilla, and Asian basil, with stems removed and leaves chopped

2 cups (200 g) bean sprouts

½ medium cucumber, core removed and julienned

3 lb (1.3 kg) fresh or cooked rice vermicelli noodles, cooled

Pickled Carrots and Daikon (page 165)

Scallion Oil (page 170)

Fish Sauce Dressing (page 167) or Vegan Dipping Sause/Dressing (page 168)

A bowl of cool rice vermicelli noodles layered on a bed of fresh greens and topped with grilled meat or seafood or crispy spring rolls is a popular dish in Vietnam. It is great to serve in the summer at outdoor barbecues. For any vermicelli bowl of this kind, you need to prepare the ingredients to the left to go with these toppings:

- Net Seafood Spring Rolls (page 109)

- Crispy Spring Rolls (page 112)

- Vegan Crispy Spring Rolls (page 114)

- Grilled Pork Skewers (page 118)

- Grilled Beef Wrapped in Wild Betel Leaf (page 119)

- Sugarcane Prawns (page 120)

NET SEAFOOD SPRING ROLLS

SKILL LEVEL: Advanced • **PREP TIME:** 45 minutes • **COOK TIME:** 45 minutes • **YIELD:** 20 rolls

INGREDIENTS

Filling

7 oz (200 g) ground meat (pork, chicken, or turkey)

7 oz (200 g) minced shrimp

½ tsp salt

½ tsp sugar, plus more to taste

½ tsp chicken or pork stock powder, plus more to taste

1 tbsp (15 ml) fish sauce

1 tbsp (10 g) minced shallot

1 tbsp (10 g) minced garlic

1 tsp black pepper, plus more to taste

7 oz (200 g) crab meat

1 cup (100 g) shredded taro

1 cup (100 g) shredded carrot

¼ cup (22 g) dried woodear mushrooms, soaked in hot water for 15 minutes, drained, excess water squeezed out, and minced

1.7 oz (50 g) glass noodles, soaked in cold water for 15 minutes, drained, and cut short

1 egg or egg white

Net Wrapper

⅔ cup (100 g) rice flour

1 tbsp plus 1 tsp (20 ml) all-purpose flour

1 tbsp plus 1 tsp (20 ml) tapioca starch

2 tbsp (30 ml) sugar

½ tbsp (8 ml) vegetable oil, plus more for frying

6 tbsp plus 2 tsp (100 ml) water

1 egg white

Serving

Accompaniments (page 108)

These rolls (*chả giò rế hải sản*) are wrapped in net wrappers, which are available at markets in Vietnam and at some Asian food stores. If you are unable to find net wrappers, you can make them yourself. In this recipe, it is crucial that you use a good nonstick pan so it is easy to remove the net wrapper in one piece. See page 115 for tips for crispier rolls.

INSTRUCTIONS

1. **To make the filling:** In a large bowl, combine the ground meat and minced shrimp. Season with the salt, ½ teaspoon sugar, ½ teaspoon chicken stock powder, fish sauce, shallot, garlic, and 1 teaspoon black pepper. Mix well in a circular motion until incorporated.

2. Gently mix in the crab meat. Add the taro, carrot, mushrooms, and glass noodles to the bowl, and mix well. To help all the ingredients adhere, add the egg. Mix well and let sit for 15 to 30 minutes.

3. **To make the net wrapper:** In a large bowl, combine the flours, tapioca starch, sugar, ½ tablespoon (8 ml) vegetable oil, water, and egg white, and stir well to dissolve completely. Let sit for about 30 minutes.

4. Heat an 8-inch (20 cm) nonstick pan over medium-low heat until warm. Dip all 5 of your fingers into the net wrapper batter, lift them up, and drizzle the batter into the pan, holding your fingers about 4 inches (10 cm) above the pan and drizzling in a crisscross motion until you create a beautiful net.

5. When the net solidifies, gently remove it and let cool. When the net wrapper is still hot, it's fragile and easy to break, but when it cools down, it will become flexible. Repeat these steps until all batter is used.

6. **To assemble the rolls:** Scoop a heaping tablespoon of filling on top of a net wrapper close to one end. Shape it nicely and then roll until you reach the center of the net wrapper. Fold both sides inward and

continued on page 110

continue to roll up until you reach the other end.

7. Fill a large pan with vegetable oil to a depth of 2 inches (5 cm). Heat the oil to 360°F (180°C), or test the temperature with a chopstick inserted into the oil: when bubbles appear around the chopstick, the oil is ready for deep-frying.

8. Gently slide the rolls into the pan, in batches with plenty of room, and fry over medium-low heat until golden brown. Remove from the pan with a slotted spoon and place on a paper towel–lined plate to drain excess oil.

9. These are best when served within 1 hour of frying. If they are left longer, you can re-fry and serve. Serve with the accompaniments on page 108.

CRISPY SPRING ROLLS

SKILL LEVEL: Intermediate • **PREP TIME:** 45 minutes • **COOK TIME:** 30 minutes • **YIELD:** 20 to 25 rolls

INGREDIENTS

7 oz (200 g) ground pork

7 oz (200 g) minced shrimp

½ tsp salt

½ tsp black pepper

½ tsp sugar plus 1 tbsp (18 ml) sugar, divided

½ tsp chicken stock powder

1 tbsp (10 g) minced shallot

1 tbsp (10 g) minced garlic

1 cup (100 g) shredded taro

1 cup (100 g) shredded carrot

¼ cup (22 g) dried woodear mushrooms, soaked in hot water for 15 minutes, drained, excess water squeezed out, and minced

1.7 oz (50 g) glass noodles, soaked in cold water for 10 minutes, drained, and cut short

1 egg or egg white

20 rice paper or spring roll wrappers

1 tbsp (15 ml) fresh lime juice

2 cups (475 ml) water

Vegetable oil, for frying

2 cups (200 g) bean sprouts (optional)

7 oz (200 g) tofu, drained well and crumbled (optional)

Accompaniments (page 108), for serving

Crispy spring rolls—called *nem rán* in northern Vietnam and *chả giò* in southern Vietnam—have become one of the most popular Vietnamese dishes the world over. Though one can vary the filling ingredients, the standard spring rolls should include ground meat, woodear mushrooms, and glass noodles for texture. The northern version adds bean sprouts and tofu, while the southern version usually has shredded taro. See page 115 for tips for crispier rolls.

INSTRUCTIONS

1. In a large bowl, combine the ground pork and minced shrimp with the salt, pepper, ½ teaspoon of the sugar, chicken stock powder, shallot, and garlic. Mix well in a circular motion until incorporated. Add the taro, carrot, mushrooms, glass noodles, bean sprouts (if using), and tofu (if using) to the bowl, and mix well. To help all the ingredients adhere, add the egg. Mix well and let sit for about 15 minutes.

2. To soften the rice paper wrappers, combine the remaining 1 tablespoon (15 ml) sugar and lime juice in the water. This will soften the rice paper and make the rolls golden brown and crispy. Wet your fingers with this liquid and spread it over the wrappers. Do not dip the wrappers in the liquid because it will make them too wet.

3. To assemble the rolls, scoop a heaping tablespoon of filling and place near one end of a rice paper wrapper. Roll until you reach the center, then fold both sides inward and continue to roll up until you reach the other end. Repeat until all filling and wrappers are used.

4. Fill a large pan with vegetable oil to a depth of 2 inches (5 cm). Heat the oil to 360°F (180°C), or test the temperature with a chopstick inserted into the oil: when bubbles appear around the chopstick, the oil is ready for deep-frying. Fry the rolls in batches of 5 to 8, depending on the size of the pan, over medium heat until golden brown. The rice paper could be sticky at first, so leave some space between the rolls. After a few minutes, you can bring them closer together. Remove from the pan with a slotted spoon and place on a paper towel–lined plate to drain the excess oil.

6. These are best when served within 1 hour of frying. If they are left longer, you can re-fry and serve. Serve with the accompaniments on page 108.

VEGAN CRISPY SPRING ROLLS

SKILL LEVEL: Intermediate • **PREP TIME:** 45 minutes • **COOK TIME:** 30 minutes • **YIELD:** 20 rolls

INGREDIENTS

½ cup (104 g) peeled split mung beans, soaked in water for 1 hour and drained

2 tbsp (30 ml) vegetable oil, plus more for frying

2 tbsp (16 g) finely chopped leek or scallion (white part only)

½ cup (44 g) straw mushrooms, finely chopped

¼ cup (22 g) dried shiitake mushrooms, soaked in water, drained, and finely chopped

½ cup (44 g) dried woodear mushrooms, soaked in water, drained, and finely chopped

1 cup (250 g) glass noodles, soaked in water for 10 minutes, drained, and chopped

1 cup (100 g) shredded taro

1 cup (100 g) shredded carrot

½ tsp salt

½ tsp black pepper

1 tsp plus 1 tbsp (20 ml) sugar, divided

1 tsp mushroom seasoning powder (optional)

20 rice paper or spring roll wrappers

1 tbsp (15 ml) fresh lime juice

2 cups (475 ml) water

Accompaniments (page 108), for serving

COOKING TIP

Frying the leek before adding it to the filling gives the roll a nice fragrance when you bite into it.

For these rolls (*chả giò chay*), I use three types of mushrooms to add texture, but you don't have to use all three. You can also use other kinds of mushrooms or vegetables that you like. Just make sure they are not watery vegetables as they may make the rolls soggy. See the opposite page for tips for crispier rolls.

INSTRUCTIONS

1. Add the soaked mung beans to a rice cooker and fill with just enough water to cover. Press to cook, 15 to 20 minutes. Alternatively, you can steam the soaked mung beans until soft. After they cook, mash them with a spoon into a paste.

2. Heat the 2 tablespoons (30 ml) vegetable oil in a small pan over medium heat. Add the leeks to the pan and cook and stir until slightly golden brown. Remove the pan from the heat.

3. In a large bowl, combine the straw, shiitake, and woodear mushrooms, along with the glass noodles, taro, carrot, and mashed mung beans. Stir in the oil from the pan that the leeks were cooked in.

4. Season with the salt, pepper, 1 teaspoon of the sugar, and mushroom seasoning powder. Mix well and let sit for about 15 minutes.

5. To soften the rice paper wrappers, combine the remaining 1 tablespoon (15 ml) sugar and lime juice in the water. This will soften the rice paper and make the rolls golden brown and crispy. Wet your fingers with this liquid and spread it over the wrappers. Do not dip the wrappers in the liquid because it will make them too wet.

6. To assemble the rolls, scoop a heaping tablespoon of filling and place near one end of a rice paper wrapper. Roll until you reach the center, then fold both sides inward and continue to roll up until you reach the other end. Repeat until all filling and wrappers are used.

7. Place a piece of parchment paper into the base of a large pan, to prevent the rolls from touching the bottom of the pan and burning, then fill with vegetable oil to a depth of 2 inches (5 cm). Heat the oil to 360°F (180°C), or test the temperature with a chopstick inserted into the oil: when bubbles appear around the chopstick, the oil is ready for deep-frying.

8. Fry the rolls in batches of 5 to 8, depending on the size of the pan, over medium heat until golden brown. The rice paper could be sticky at first, so leave some space between the rolls. After a few minutes, you can bring them closer together. Remove from the pan with a slotted spoon and place on a paper towel–lined plate to drain the excess oil.

9. These are best when served within 1 hour of frying. If they are left longer, you can re-fry and serve. Serve with the accompaniments on page 108.

TIPS FOR CRISPIER SPRING ROLLS

A good spring roll should be evenly golden and crispy, and will stay that way even after a few hours. The filling should be succulent, but not soggy. Here are some tips to help you achieve the best results when making Net Seafood Spring Rolls (page 109), Crispy Spring Rolls (page 112), and Vegan Crispy Spring Rolls.

WRAPPING
It shows off your technique when you can produce a crispy spring roll, one that is neither too sticky nor too sloppy. If you want to make authentic Vietnamese spring rolls, they should be wrapped with rice paper.

- Do not soak rice paper in water, as it becomes too soft and wet to work with; instead, slightly wet the cutting board and place the rice paper on top. By the time you finish spooning on the filling, it should be soft enough to roll. Alternatively, place the rice paper inside a folded, damp cloth for a couple of seconds.
- For nice and evenly golden-brown rolls, use Coca-Cola, Sarsi (a Southeast Asian sarsaparilla soft drink), beer, or coconut water instead of water to wet the rice paper. The sugar content in these liquids caramelizes under high oil temperatures, browning the rolls nicely.
- When you're done wrapping, roll each spring roll back and forth under your palm on the counter to release the air bubbles inside. This prevents bubbles from forming on the skin of the rolls.
- Place the rolls in the refrigerator for 2 hours before frying, so the rice paper has time to dry.

FILLING
Some vegetable filling ingredients might release their juices during frying, which leaves the rolls not so crispy. To prevent this, mix such ingredients with some sugar—1 tablespoon (15 ml) per 2 cups (200 g) vegetables—and squeeze out the excess moisture after letting them sit for 15 minutes.

FRYING
- Make sure there is enough frying oil to fully cover the rolls.
- Add a few drops of fresh lime juice to the frying oil before it is heated to make the rolls crispier.
- Fry over medium-low heat—the temperature of the oil should be 300 to 320°F (150 to 160°C) after the rolls are added to the oil.
- Double frying is always the secret to keeping fried food crispy for a long time. First, fry over medium-low heat to cook the fillings, and then fry again over medium-high heat to brown the roll.
- You can freeze the rolls after the first fry, but do not defrost for the second fry; just drop them into the oil frozen.
- After frying, drain off excess oil by standing the rolls up on a frying rack or placing them on paper towels. Do not turn off the heat and leave the rolls in oil; they will turn soggy.

BEEF VERMICELLI NOODLE SALAD

SKILL LEVEL: Easy • **PREP TIME:** 15 minutes • **COOK TIME:** 10 minutes • **YIELD:** 4 to 6 servings

INGREDIENTS

1 lb (454 g) beef (rumpsteak, sirloin, or eye of round), thinly sliced against the grain

1 tbsp (18 g) oyster sauce (optional)

1 tbsp (10 g) minced garlic, divided

1 tbsp (8 g) minced lemongrass

½ tsp salt

½ tsp black pepper

1 tsp chicken stock powder or sugar

3 tbsp (45 ml) vegetable oil, divided

1 head leaf or iceberg lettuce, leaves torn into small pieces or shredded

3 lb (1.3 kg) fresh or cooked rice vermicelli noodles, cooled

½ cup Pickled Carrots and Daikon (page 165)

¼ cup (40 g) crispy fried shallot (*hành phi*; you can buy these at an Asian food store)

¼ cup (36 g) crushed roasted peanuts

Fish Sauce Dressing (page 167)

This salad (*bún bò Nam Bộ*) is easy to make and a refreshing summer delight. It's a great dish for introducing someone to Vietnamese cuisine. Most of my Western friends love it, as it's healthy and full of flavor.

INSTRUCTIONS

1. In a large bowl, combine the beef, oyster sauce (if using), ½ tablespoon (5 g) of the garlic, lemongrass, salt, black pepper, chicken stock powder, and 1 tablespoon (15 ml) of the vegetable oil. Mix well and let marinate for at least 15 minutes.

2. Heat the remaining 2 tablespoons (30 ml) vegetable oil in a large wok or pan over high heat—let it get nice and hot. Add the remaining ½ tablespoon (5 g) garlic and cook and stir until fragrant. Add the marinated beef and stir-fry over high heat until the beef is no longer pink on the outside.

3. To assemble the dish, place the lettuce in a large serving bowl, followed by a handful of cold rice vermicelli noodles. Top with the stir-fried beef, Pickled Carrots and Daikon, fried shallot, and crushed peanuts.

4. Toss with some Fish Sauce Dressing and serve.

COOKING TIP

It is crucial that you slice the beef very thinly against the grain. Make sure you turn the heat on high when stir-frying, but don't overcook the meat. Stir-fry just until the color changes, then serve immediately, as the beef tends to discolor after a short while.

GRILLED PORK SKEWERS

SKILL LEVEL: Advanced • **PREP TIME:** 1 hour • **COOK TIME:** 25 minutes • **YIELD:** 12 skewers (4 servings)

INGREDIENTS

1⅓ lb (600 g) ground pork (see Shopping Tip, below)

2 tbsp (30 ml) fish sauce

1 tsp chicken stock powder

½ tsp salt

1 tsp black pepper

1 tbsp plus 1 tsp sugar (20 ml), divided

2 tbsp (30 ml) cornstarch or tapioca starch

½ tsp baking powder

2 tbsp (30 ml) Annatto Oil (page 170)

3½ oz (100 g) pork lard, diced

4 shallots, peeled

1 head garlic, peeled

Vegetable oil, for greasing

12 bamboo skewers, soaked in water and two-thirds upper part rolled over cornstarch

Accompaniments (page 108), for serving

When making this dish (*nem nướng*), **the seasoned meat is pounded by hand using a traditional method called** *quết*. **It helps make the meat paste stickier, so it will bind together for a chewy and springy texture when cooked. Another technique we use is called** *đập thịt*, **meaning you pick up the paste and—bang!—throw it back in the bowl. Repeat about twenty times.**

INSTRUCTIONS

1. In a large bowl, combine the ground pork, fish sauce, chicken stock powder, salt, black pepper, 1 tablespoon (15 ml) of the sugar, cornstarch, baking powder, and Annatto Oil. Mix well and let marinate for 30 minutes. Put the seasoned pork in the freezer for about 30 minutes before processing in step 3.

2. Soak the pork lard in boiling water for 10 minutes. Drain well and combine with the remaining 1 teaspoon sugar.

3. Using a food processor, finely blend the shallots and garlic. Take the seasoned pork out of the freezer and pulse to grind in the food processor with the shallots and garlic, until it becomes a solid paste. Give the food processor a 15-second break after every 15 seconds of processing.

4. Grease a mortar and pestle with vegetable oil to prevent sticking. Hand-pound the seasoned pork in the mortar steadily for 5 minutes.

5. Combine the seasoned pork paste with the pork lard. Transfer the mixture to a resealable plastic bag and cut the tip off one of the bottom corners.

6. Insert the cornstarch end of the skewer into the hole and continuously squeeze out the pork mixture. Shape nicely to help the meat stick to the skewer. Repeat this step until you use all the meat.

7. Arrange the pork skewers on a grilling rack. Grill for 7 to 10 minutes, until the meat solidifies, then turn the skewers over. Brush both sides with a shiny coat of Annatto Oil. Grill for another 7 to 10 minutes. You can also use a charcoal grill or cook in an oven at 400°F (200°C) for about 20 to 25 minutes, flipping halfway through.

8. Serve with the accompaniments on page 108.

SHOPPING TIP

It is important to use very fresh meat (best butchered the same day) for this recipe and have it ground by the butcher or do it yourself at home. Fresh meat is stickier once ground and even more so after *quết* and *đập thịt*.

GRILLED BEEF WRAPPED IN WILD BETEL LEAF

SKILL LEVEL: Intermediate • **PREP TIME:** 30 minutes • **COOK TIME:** 30 minutes • **YIELD:** 4 to 6 servings

INGREDIENTS

1 lb (454 g) beef (rumpsteak, sirloin, or eye of round), minced or thinly sliced against the grain

3½ oz (100 g) pork fatback, diced

1 tsp salt

1 tsp sugar

1 tsp chicken stock powder

½ tsp black pepper

1 tbsp (10 g) minced garlic

1 tbsp (10 g) minced shallot

3 tbsp (24 g) minced lemongrass

1 tsp five-spice powder (optional)

3 tbsp (27 g) crushed roasted peanuts, plus more for serving (3 tbsp, or 27 g, are optional)

1 bunch wild betel leaves (30 to 35 pieces), stems trimmed to 1 inch (2.5 cm) long, rinsed, and patted dry

10 to 15 bamboo skewers

Vegetable oil, for brushing

Scallion Oil (page 170)

Anchovy Dipping Sauce (page 168; optional)

Accompaniments (page 108), for serving

Before you get all confused about the betel leaf used in this dish (*bò lá lốt*), the leaf we use is wild betel leaf (*piper sarmentosum*, or *lá lốt*), and not the betel leaf that can be chewed with areca as a mouth freshener (a.k.a. piper betel, or *lá trầu*). They are completely different leaves. Only wild betel leaf gives off a stunning fragrance when you put it on the grill. If you can't find wild betel leaf, you should substitute grape leaf, not piper betel leaf.

INSTRUCTIONS

1. In a large bowl, combine the beef, fatback, salt, sugar, chicken stock powder, black pepper, garlic, shallot, lemongrass, five-spice powder (if using), and 3 tablespoons (27 g) peanuts (if using). Let marinate for 30 minutes.

2. To wrap, place a betel leaf on a flat surface with the shiny, darker side facing down and the stem pointing out. Place 1 tablespoon of the meat mixture near the tip of the leaf and shape it into a small log across the leaf for easy rolling. Cover the meat with the tip and roll it up like a cigar, stopping when you almost reach the stem.

3. Punch a tiny hole with the tip of a skewer or a toothpick in the middle of the roll, then insert the leaf stem into the hole to secure. You can place a few rolls onto one skewer.

4. Grill outdoors over charcoal for 10 minutes or cook in an oven at 350°F (180°C) for 15 to 20 minutes. Brush the rolls with vegetable oil before and during grilling so they don't dry up and every 10 minutes if cooking in the oven. Alternatively, you can fry them in 3 tablespoons (45 ml) vegetable oil in a pan over medium heat for 2 to 3 minutes per side. Whether grilling or frying, you might need to open one to see if it is cooked inside.

5. Top with crushed peanuts and Scallion Oil.

6. Serve with Anchovy Dipping Sauce (if using) and the accompaniments on page 108.

SUGARCANE PRAWNS

SKILL LEVEL: Intermediate • **PREP TIME:** 40 minutes • **COOK TIME:** 15 minutes • **YIELD:** 2 to 4 servings

INGREDIENTS

1 lb (454 g) tiger prawns, peeled and deveined

1.76 oz (50 g) pork paste (*giò sống*; optional)

½ tsp salt

½ tsp black pepper

½ tsp sugar

½ tsp chicken stock powder

1 tbsp (15 ml) fish sauce

1 scallion, white part minced and green part chopped

Vegetable oil, for greasing

6-inch (15 cm) piece sugarcane, split into 10 to 12 thin sticks

Accompaniments (page 108), for serving

Pork paste adds a firmer texture to the shrimp in this dish (*chạo tôm*), but you can also skip it if it's not available. Pork paste, or *giò sống*, is a popular item in wet markets in Vietnam. Freshly butchered pork is ground and pounded into a sticky paste. Some Asian stores offer pork paste in frozen form. You can grind and pound fresh meat yourself at home, too. Apply the *đập thịt* and *quết* techniques used in the Grilled Pork Skewers (page 118).

INSTRUCTIONS

1. Using a food processor, grind the prawns into a fine paste. Mix with the pork paste (if using), until well combined.

2. Season the paste with the salt, black pepper, sugar, chicken stock powder, fish sauce, and minced scallion. Mix well.

3. To increase the stickiness, wearing plastic gloves, pick up the paste and throw it back into the bowl with strength. Repeat 20 times.

4. Remove gloves and grease clean hands with vegetable oil. Pinch off about 3 tablespoons of the paste and wrap it around a sugarcane stick to cover two-thirds of its length, leaving the remaining one-third clean for handling. Press to stick the paste to the sugarcane as securely as possible. Repeat until all paste is used.

5. There are two options for cooking: frying or grilling. To fry, fill a large pan with vegetable oil to a depth of 2 in (5 cm). Heat until the oil reaches 300°F (150°C), or test the temperature with a chopstick inserted into the oil: when bubbles appear around the chopstick, the oil is ready for frying. Fry until golden brown. If grilling, steam the prawn skewers for 5 minutes to preserve their shape, then grill over medium heat to get grill marks.

6. Serve with the accompaniments on page 108.

SHOPPING TIP

Sugarcane adds natural sweetness to the shrimp and pork paste. You can buy sugarcane sticks in a can at Asian food stores.

GRILLED PORK WITH VERMICELLI NOODLES AND FRESH GREENS

SKILL LEVEL: Intermediate • **PREP TIME:** 30 minutes • **COOK TIME:** 30 minutes • **YIELD:** 6 to 8 servings

INGREDIENTS

Pork

1 lb (454 g) pork belly or pork shoulder, thinly sliced

4 tbsp (40 g) minced garlic, divided

4 tbsp (40 g) minced shallot, divided

2 tbsp (36 g) oyster sauce, divided (optional)

2 tbsp (25 g) sugar, divided

4 tbsp (60 ml) fish sauce, divided

4 tbsp (52 g) caramel sauce (see Cooking Tip, opposite) or 2 tbsp (40 g) molasses or honey, divided

2 tsp pork stock powder, divided, (optional)

1 tsp ground black pepper, divided

1 lb (454 g) ground pork

Pickles

1 cup (135 g) thinly sliced kohlrabi or green papaya (bite-size pieces)

2 medium carrots, thinly sliced into rounds

2 tsp salt

1 tbsp (15 ml) sugar

2 tbsp (30 ml) rice vinegar (5 percent acidity)

In central and southern Vietnam, we have a dish of grilled pork and vermicelli that is similar to this dish (*bún chả*); it is called *bún thịt nướng* (Grilled Pork Vermicelli Noodle Salad on page 127). But as soon as I discovered *bún chả*, it became my favorite dish from Hanoi. Rather than serving everything in one bowl, *bún chả* is served as a separate bowl of dipping sauce alongside grilled pork and a platter of fresh greens and vermicelli noodles.

INSTRUCTIONS

1. **To make the pork:** In a large bowl, combine the pork belly with 2 tablespoons (20 g) of the garlic, 2 tablespoons (20 g) of the shallot, 1 tablespoon (18 g) of the oyster sauce (if using), 1 tablespoon (13 g) of the sugar, 2 tablespoons (30 ml) of the fish sauce, 2 tablespoons (26 g) of the caramel sauce, 1 teaspoon of the pork stock powder (if using), and ½ teaspoon of the black pepper. Cover and marinate in the refrigerator for at least 30 minutes or a few hours.

2. In a separate large bowl, combine the ground pork with the remaining 2 tablespoons (20 g) garlic, 2 tablespoons (20 g) shallot, 1 tablespoon (18 g) oyster sauce (if using), 1 tablespoon (12 g) sugar, 2 tablespoons (30 ml) fish sauce, 2 tablespoons (26 g) caramel sauce, 1 teaspoon pork stock powder (if using), and ½ teaspoon of black pepper. Cover and let marinate in the refrigerator for at least 30 minutes or a few hours.

3. Pinch and form the ground pork into 2-inch (5 cm) patties.

4. Grill the pork belly and ground pork patties outdoors over charcoal until both sides are golden brown, about 20 minutes, flipping halfway through. Alternatively, you can "grill" in the oven: Line a baking sheet with foil and place an oven rack on top. Set another oven rack to the upper third of the oven. Distribute the meat on the rack on the baking sheet and place the sheet in the oven. Bake at 350°F (175°C) for 30 minutes, flipping halfway through.

Dipping Sauce

½ cup (120 ml) fish sauce

½ cup (100 g) sugar

3 cups (700 ml) water

1 tbsp (10 g) minced garlic

1 tbsp (9 g) minced bird's eye chili peppers

Serving

3 lb (1.3 kg) fresh or cooked rice vermicelli noodles, cooled

1 head leaf or iceberg lettuce, leaves torn into small pieces or shredded

COOKING TIP

You can cook the pork indoors on a grill pan or in a nonstick pan. In this case, add 1 tablespoon (15 ml) vegetable oil to the marinade, and only grill a few pieces of pork at a time. If you overcrowd the meat, you will get *thit kho* (caramelized pork) instead of grilled pork.

To make the caramel sauce, melt ¼ cup (50 g) of sugar in a heavy-bottom saucepan over medium heat until caramelized, occasionally swirling the pan to avoid burning. Take the pan off the heat. Using a long-handle ladle, add 2 tablespoons (30 ml) of hot water to the caramelized sugar. Be careful, as it will splash.

5. **To make the pickles:** In a large bowl, combine the kohlrabi and carrots with the salt. Let sit for 15 minutes. Rinse well and lightly squeeze out the excess water.

6. In a large bowl, combine the kohlrabi and carrots with the sugar and vinegar. Let sit for at least 1 hour so that the vegetables can absorb the flavors.

7. **To make the dipping sauce:** Add the fish sauce, sugar, and water to a medium saucepan over medium-low heat. Cook until the sugar dissolves. Minced garlic and chili peppers can be added to taste while serving.

8. **To assemble the dish:** Fill a medium serving bowl half-full with the dipping sauce, some grilled pork, pickles, minced garlic, and minced chili peppers. Season with black pepper.

9. Dip some vermicelli noodles and fresh greens into the dipping sauce and eat with the grilled pork and pickles.

VERMICELLI NOODLE SALAD BOWL WITH ROASTED PORK AND ANCHOVY SAUCE

SKILL LEVEL: Intermediate • **PREP TIME:** 30 minutes • **COOK TIME:** 1 hour • **YIELD:** 12 servings

INGREDIENTS

Roasted Pork
2¼ lb (1 kg) pork belly, rinsed and patted dry

2 tsp sugar

1 tsp five-spice powder

½ tsp black pepper

1 tbsp (16 g) hoisin sauce or ketchup (optional)

3 tsp salt, divided

1 tsp white vinegar

Toppings
10½ oz (300 g) young unripe jackfruit (this can be bought in a can at Asian food stores; optional)

7 oz (200 g) green papaya, shredded (optional)

Serving
1 head leaf or iceberg lettuce, leaves torn into small pieces or shredded

3 sprigs each of herbs such as mint, perilla, and Asian basil, with stems removed and leaves chopped

3 lb (1.3 kg) fresh or cooked rice vermicelli noodles, cooled

2 to 3 tbsp (30 to 45 ml) Annatto Oil (page 170)

Anchovy Dipping Sauce (page 168)

¼ cup (36 g) crushed roasted peanuts

¼ cup (40 g) crispy fried shallot (*hành phi*; you can buy these at an Asian food store)

This dish (*bún mắm nêm thịt heo quay*) **is without a doubt my all-time favorite food. I often joke with my friends that every time I fly home to Da Nang, I visit the** *bún mắm* **vendor before visiting my parents. Believe it or not, the joke has been proven true more than once! This recipe for roasted pork is the simplest you will find, and it always turns out so well. For a large piece of pork, one popular technique to help the pork skin bubble more easily and get crispy is to use a skewer to poke through the skin as much as possible in step 6. However, you can skip the poking for smaller pork pieces; they will crisp up on their own.**

INSTRUCTIONS

1. **To make the roasted pork:** Slice incisions, about ⅓ inch (8.5 mm) deep, along the length of the pork. Space the incisions 1 inch (2.5 cm) apart.

2. In a small bowl, combine the sugar, five-spice powder, black pepper, hoisin sauce (if using), and 1 teaspoon of the salt.

3. Rub this mixture over all sides of the pork except the skin. Place the pork, skin side up, on a plate and use paper towels to wipe the skin clean and dry.

4. In another small bowl, combine the remaining 2 teaspoons salt with the vinegar. Brush one-third of this mixture onto the pork skin. Let marinate in the refrigerator for 3 hours or overnight.

5. Preheat the oven to 400°F (200°C). Place the pork, skin side down, on a baking tray lined with aluminum foil. Roast for 20 minutes.

6. Remove from the oven and turn the pork over so the skin side is facing up. Use paper towels to wipe the skin dry. To help the skin bubble and crisp up, poke all over with a fork or skewer. Brush the skin with half of the remaining salt-vinegar mixture. Roast for another 20 minutes.

continued on page 126

COOKING TIP

The vinegar and salt are vital to making the skin dry and crispy. You don't have to use up the mixture, but make sure you spread on enough to help the skin bubble. If the skin is too salty, you can scrape some off once it is cooked.

7. You will see bubbles start to appear on the skin. Take the pork out of the oven, wipe the fat off the skin, and brush with the remaining salt-vinegar mixture. Roast for a final 20 minutes—the total cook time is 60 minutes.

8. **To make the toppings:** Place the young jackfruit (if using) in a large saucepan filled with enough water to cover. Bring to a boil, reduce the heat to medium, and cook until it is soft enough that you can cut through it with a spoon, about 30 minutes. It might take less time if you use canned young jackfruit. Let cool, then julienne the jackfruit along the grain.

9. To assemble the bowls, add some fresh greens and herbs to the serving bowls and top with cold rice vermicelli noodles. Add the roasted pork, jackfruit (if using) and/or green papaya (if using), Annatto Oil, and the Anchovy Dipping Sauce. Garnish with crushed peanuts and fried shallot, and mix well.

GRILLED PORK VERMICELLI NOODLE SALAD

SKILL LEVEL: Intermediate • **PREP TIME:** 30 minutes • **COOK TIME:** 30 minutes • **YIELD:** 4 servings

INGREDIENTS

3 tbsp (24 g) minced lemongrass
1 tbsp (10 g) minced garlic
1 tbsp (10 g) minced shallot
½ tsp black pepper
2 tbsp (30 ml) soy sauce
1 tbsp (15 ml) fish sauce
2 tbsp (36 g) oyster sauce
1 tbsp (20 g) honey
1 tbsp (15 ml) sugar
1 tbsp (8 g) sesame seeds
2 tbsp (30 ml) vegetable oil
1 lb (454 g) pork shoulder or pork belly, thinly sliced
1 head leaf or iceberg lettuce, leaves torn into small pieces or shredded
3 sprigs each of herbs such as mint, perilla, and Asian basil, with stems removed and leaves chopped
3 lb (1.3 kg) fresh or cooked rice vermicelli noodles, cooled
Pickled Carrots and Daikon (page 165)
½ medium cucumber, core removed and julienned
Fish Sauce Dressing (page 167) or Central-Style Peanut Liver Sauce (page 161)
¼ cup (40 g) crispy fried shallot (*hành phi*; you can buy these at an Asian food store)

In southern Vietnam, this dish (*bún thịt nướng*) uses the Fish Sauce Dressing (page 167). In central Vietnam, the Central-Style Peanut Liver Sauce (page 161) enriches the flavor. It is common to find Crispy Spring Rolls (page 112) or Beef Wrapped in Wild Betel Leaf (page 119) added to this bowl.

INSTRUCTIONS

1. In a large bowl, combine the lemongrass, garlic, shallot, black pepper, soy sauce, fish sauce, oyster sauce, honey, sugar, sesame seeds, and vegetable oil. Add the pork to the bowl and mix well. Cover and let marinate in the refrigerator for 2 to 3 hours or overnight.

2. Grill the pork outside over charcoal using a grilling basket, cooking 7 minutes on each side, or skewer and roast in a 400°F (200°C) oven for 20 to 25 minutes. If the meat gets too dry, brush some vegetable oil on top.

3. Place a layer of fresh greens and herbs at the base of the bowl and top with cold rice vermicelli noodles. Add the grilled pork, Pickled Carrots and Daikon, cucumber, your dressing of choice, and fried shallot. Mix well.

EVEN MORE NOODLE SOUPS AND DISHES

Các món sợi khác

HOI AN-STYLE NOODLES WITH PORK AND GREENS

SKILL LEVEL: Intermediate • **PREP TIME:** 20 minutes • **COOK TIME:** 1 hour 15 minutes • **YIELD:** 4 to 6 servings

INGREDIENTS

Char Siu (Roasted Pork)

7 cloves garlic, pounded to a paste
  in a mortar and pestle
2 tbsp (30 ml) soy sauce
1 tsp five-spice powder
½ tsp salt (optional)
1 tsp sugar
1 tsp pork or chicken stock powder
½ tsp black pepper
1 lb (454 g) pork shoulder
Vegetable oil, for frying

Broth

2¼ lb (1 kg) pork bones
12 cups (3 qt, or 3 L) water
1 tsp salt, plus more to taste
1 medium yellow onion, peeled
Sugar, to taste
Chicken stock powder, to taste

SHOPPING TIP

I use pork shoulder because it's lean with just a little fat to keep the meat juicy. You can also use pork thigh, belly, or loin. Searing with a generous amount of oil helps prevent the pork skin from spitting.

The noodles for this dish (*cao lầu*) are made from rice soaked in lye water, which gives them a nice chewy, springy texture and a grayish-brown color. Legend has it that the water has to be from the Bá Lễ Well, and the lye has to be obtained by leaching the ashes of particular plants on Cu Lao Cham Island (10 miles, or 16 km, from Hoi An). This is the reason why you can't really find this dish anywhere outside this ancient town. Dried *cao lầu* noodles are not available overseas either. Substitute with Italian whole-grain linguine or Japanese soba noodles instead.

INSTRUCTIONS

1. **To make the Central Vietnam-style char siu:** In a large bowl, combine the garlic, soy sauce, five-spice powder, salt (if using), sugar, pork stock powder, and black pepper. Add the pork to the bowl and massage the marinade on all sides. Cover and let marinate in the refrigerator for at least 30 minutes, but preferably 2 to 3 hours or overnight.

2. **To make the broth:** Place the pork bones in a large stockpot. Fill with enough water to cover them. Bring to a boil and cook for 5 to 10 minutes, until the impurities rise to the top. Drain the pot and rinse the bones well under running water to wash off the impurities.

3. Place the bones in a large stockpot and fill with the water. (If you use the same pot as in step 2, make sure you clean it before putting the bones back. It is crucial for a clear broth.) Add the 1 teaspoon salt and onion. Bring to a boil and skim off the scum. Reduce the heat to medium-low and simmer, uncovered, for 1 hour. Occasionally skim off the scum. If the broth reduces, add hot water to compensate, making sure you always have the same amount as when you started.

4. In a large wok or pan, add vegetable oil to a depth of 1 inch (2.5 cm). Heat until the oil reaches 360°F (180°C), or test the temperature with a chopstick inserted into the oil: when bubbles appear around the chopstick, the oil is ready for deep-frying.

continued on page 132

Noodle Bowl

1 head leaf lettuce, shredded

Fresh herbs such as mint, perilla, lemon basil, coriander, chrysanthemum, bitter mint, and fish mint

1 lb (454 g) bean sprouts, blanched

2¼ lb (1 kg) *cao lầu* noodles (you can substitute Italian whole-grain linguine or Japanese soba noodles)

½ cup (125 g) *cao lầu* crispy squares (you can substitute dried lasagna sheets cut into 1-inch, or 2.5 cm, squares), deep-fried or microwaved for 1 minute

1 lime, cut into wedges

Sweet chili sauce

5. Scrape the garlic off the marinated pork, back into the marinade. Reserve the marinade. Gently slide the pork into the oil and sear both sides over medium-high heat, about 5 minutes per side.

6. After searing, extract the oil (and burnt garlic, if any) from the wok and discard. Keep the pork in the same wok and add the saved marinade and ¼ cup (60 ml) of the pork broth. Simmer over low heat for 30 to 45 minutes. Occasionally flip the pork so it is well coated with the sauce. You can also cover the wok to shorten the cooking time. The pork is cooked through when you pierce it with a chopstick and the juice coming out runs clear, not pink. When cooked, transfer the pork to a plate and let it cool. Thinly slice it into bite-size pieces.

7. Transfer the pork broth from the stockpot to the wok with the marinade and combine. Discard the pork bones. Season to taste with salt, sugar, and chicken stock powder, making sure the broth is a bit saltier than a soup.

8. **To assemble the noodle bowls:** Fill the serving bowls half-full with fresh lettuce, herbs, and bean sprouts. Place the noodles on top. Top with sliced *char siu* pork and ladle the broth over, just enough to wet the noodles.

9. Serve with the crispy squares, lime wedges, and sweet chili sauce. Stir well before serving.

GLASS NOODLE SOUP WITH CHICKEN

SKILL LEVEL: Easy • **PREP TIME:** 20 minutes • **COOK TIME:** 1 hour • **YIELD:** 4 servings

INGREDIENTS

1 whole chicken (about 2½ lb, or 1.2 kg)

1 tbsp (15 ml) salt, plus more for the chicken and to taste

1 scallion

4 slices ginger (cut lengthwise into ⅛-in-thick, or 3 mm, slices), divided

2 small yellow onions, peeled and halved, divided

6 shallots (3 kept whole and 3 thinly sliced), divided

5 coriander roots

1 set chicken internal organs (liver, heart, gizzard), rinsed and thinly sliced (optional)

½ tsp fish sauce, plus more for serving (optional)

½ tsp black pepper, plus more to taste (optional)

½ tsp chicken stock powder, plus more to taste (½ tsp is optional)

1 tsp minced shallot (optional)

3 kaffir lime leaves, rolled and sliced into fine threads

Sugar, to taste

1 tbsp (15 ml) vegetable oil

14 oz (400 g) glass noodles, soaked in warm water for 10 minutes and drained

½ cup (30 g) chopped Vietnamese mint

1 lime, cut into wedges, for serving

3 bird's eye chili peppers, thinly sliced on the bias, for serving

This soup (*miến gà*) **is simple to cook and doesn't require too many herbs or sauces. It is a hearty noodle soup I like to prepare for breakfast on the weekend. The internal organs that come with a fresh chicken are a treasure. What a waste if you throw them away. Stir-fry them for the soup; you won't believe the depth of flavor!**

INSTRUCTIONS

1. Rub the chicken with salt. Optional: Rinse the chicken well under cold running water, inside and out. Insert the scallion and 2 slices of the ginger into its cavity.

2. Add the chicken to a stockpot. Fill with enough water to cover it. Add the 1 tablespoon (15 ml) salt and one of the onions. Bring to a boil, then skim off the scum, if any. Reduce the heat to low and simmer, uncovered. Occasionally skim off the scum. Depending on the type of chicken, it may take from 15 minutes to an hour to cook. If the broth reduces, add hot water to compensate, making sure you always have the same amount as when you started.

3. Heat the remaining onion, remaining 2 ginger slices, 3 whole shallots, and coriander roots directly over an open flame on the stove until slightly charred on all sides. Peel the onion and shallots, then rinse the onion, shallots, ginger, and coriander under warm running water and scrape off the charred bits. Place all these ingredients in a spice ball or large tea or spice bag(s), or wrap securely in a piece of cheesecloth, then add to the stockpot to enhance the aroma.

4. If using internal organs, season with ½ teaspoon each of the fish sauce, black pepper, and chicken stock powder, along with the minced shallot. Set aside.

5. When you pierce the meat with a chopstick and see no pink water coming out, it is cooked. Remove the chicken from the stockpot and let cool. Shred the meat into thin strips. Lightly season the shredded chicken with salt, black pepper, and the lime leaf threads.

6. For a heartier broth, return the chicken bones to the stockpot and cook for an additional 30 to 60 minutes. Season to taste with salt, sugar, and chicken stock powder (if using).

7. Heat the vegetable oil in a large wok or pan over medium heat. Add the sliced shallots and fry until golden brown. Keep the heat on medium and immediately remove the fried shallots with a slotted spoon and transfer to a small bowl. Set aside.

8. Add the internal organs (if using) to the oil in the pan and stir-fry over high heat until cooked, about 2 minutes.

9. To assemble the bowls, add a handful of the softened glass noodles to each serving bowl. Top with the shredded chicken, fried shallots, and some chopped Vietnamese mint. Ladle the hot soup over the chicken and noodles. Add the stir-fried chicken organs if you like.

10. Serve with the lime wedges, chili pepper slices, and extra fish sauce (if using).

GLASS NOODLE SOUP WITH EEL

SKILL LEVEL: Intermediate • **PREP TIME:** 45 minutes • **COOK TIME:** 1 hour 30 minutes • **YIELD:** 6 servings

INGREDIENTS

Broth
2¼ lb (1 kg) pork bones
1 tbsp (15 ml) rice vinegar
12 cups (3 qt, or 3 L) water
1 tbsp (15 ml) salt, plus more to
   taste
1 tsp rock sugar
1 medium yellow onion, peeled and
   halved
5 shallots (2 kept whole and 3 thinly
   sliced), divided
2 slices ginger (cut lengthwise into
   ⅛-inch-thick, or 3 mm, slices)
Fish sauce, to taste
Chicken stock powder, to taste

Eel
4 cups (1 qt, or 1 L) water
1 tsp salt, divided
1 lb (454 g) eel
½ tsp black pepper
½ tsp turmeric powder
½ tsp grated ginger
½ cup (60 g) cornstarch
Vegetable oil, for frying

Noodle Bowl
14 oz (400 g) glass noodles, soaked
   in warm water for
   10 minutes and drained
½ cup (30 g) chopped
   Vietnamese mint
Black pepper, to taste
3 scallions (green parts chopped;
   white parts kept whole, smashed,
   and blanched)
Black pepper, to taste
3 bird's eye chili peppers, thinly
   sliced on the bias
2 limes, cut into wedges
Fish sauce

In restaurants in Vietnam that serve this dish (*miến lươn*), you can choose soft eel (*lươn mềm*) or crispy eel (*lươn giòn*). I combine both versions in this recipe, but feel free to cook just one of them.

INSTRUCTIONS

1. **To make the broth:** Place the pork bones in a large stockpot. Fill with enough water to cover them. Add the vinegar and bring to a boil. Cook for 5 to 10 minutes, until the impurities rise to the top. Drain the pot and rinse the bones well under running water to wash off the impurities.

2. Place the bones in a large stockpot and fill with the water. (If you use the same pot as in step 1, make sure you clean it before putting the bones back. It is crucial for a clear broth.) Add the 1 tablespoon (15 ml) salt, rock sugar, and onion. Bring to a boil and skim off the scum. Reduce the heat to medium-low and simmer, uncovered, for 1 to 2 hours. Occasionally skim off the scum. If the broth reduces, add hot water to compensate, making sure you always have the same amount as when you started.

3. Heat the 2 whole shallots and ginger slices directly over an open flame on the stove until slightly charred on all sides. Peel the shallots, then rinse the shallots and ginger under warm running water and scrape off the charred bits. Place all these ingredients in a spice ball or large tea or spice bag(s), or wrap securely in a piece of cheesecloth, then add to the stockpot during the last hour of cooking to enhance the aroma.

4. **To make the eel:** Add the water and ½ teaspoon of the salt to a small saucepan, and bring to a boil. Add the eels and cook for 2 to 5 minutes depending on their size. When you see cracks on the eels' backs, they are cooked. Remove from the saucepan and let cool. Reserve the water in the saucepan.

5. Hold the heads of the eels with one hand, and use the thumb, index, and middle finger of the other hand to pull the flesh off the bone. If using large eels, you can fillet the flesh with a knife.

You can buy packages of frozen eel at Asian food stores. Normally, these are much bigger than the ones we buy in Vietnam, and they're already cut up and cleaned. In Vietnam, we buy live eels at the wet markets, choosing ones with yellow bellies. They're from the rice fields, not home-raised, and have tastier flesh. To prepare fresh eel, we rub salt and lime juice along the body to reduce the gamey smell and sliminess. We remove the guts, and then rinse well with warm salted water.

6. Bring the reserved water in the saucepan to a boil. Crush the eel bones in a mortar and pestle, add to the reserved water in the saucepan, and boil for another 15 minutes to release the sweetness. Strain to extract the eel broth. Set aside.

7. Gather the eel flesh in a medium bowl and combine with the remaining ½ teaspoon salt, black pepper, turmeric powder, and ginger. Divide into 2 parts, setting one part aside.

8. Spread the cornstarch on a plate and coat the sliced shallots and the other part of the seasoned eel in the cornstarch.

9. Place a small pan over medium heat. Fill with vegetable oil to a depth of 2 inches (5 cm). Heat until the oil reaches 360°F (180°C), or test the temperature with a chopstick inserted into the oil: when bubbles appear around the chopstick, the oil is ready for deep-frying. Fry the sliced shallots over medium heat until golden brown. Remove with a slotted spoon and transfer to a small bowl. Set aside.

10. In the same pan, fry the eel over medium heat until golden brown, about 2 minutes. Remove with a slotted spoon and place on a paper towel–lined plate to drain the excess oil.

11. Transfer the pork broth to another stockpot and pour in the eel broth. Season to taste with fish sauce and chicken stock powder. Bring the broth to a boil.

12. **To assemble the noodle bowls:** For each bowl, place a handful of soaked glass noodles into a noodle strainer and submerge into the boiling broth to blanch. Transfer the noodles to serving bowls. Top with some soft eel and crispy fried eel, Vietnamese mint, chopped scallions, blanched scallions, and black pepper. Ladle the hot soup over the eel and noodles, then top with fried shallots and chili pepper slices.

13. Serve with the lime wedges and fish sauce for dipping.

QUANG-STYLE NOODLE WITH PORK AND SHRIMP

SKILL LEVEL: Intermediate • **PREP TIME:** 1 hour • **COOK TIME:** 45 minutes • **YIELD:** 10 servings

INGREDIENTS

1 lb (454 g) pork belly, thinly sliced

1 tbsp (10 g) minced shallot

1¼ tsp turmeric powder, divided (¼ tsp is optional)

1 tsp salt, divided, plus more to taste

1 tsp black pepper, divided

3 tbsp (45 ml) fish sauce, divided, plus more to taste

1 lb (454 g) white shrimp, shell-on, with legs, heads, and tails trimmed

4 tbsp (60 ml) vegetable oil, divided

1 tbsp (10 g) minced garlic

1 lb (454 g) fresh tomatoes, peeled, seeds removed, and pureed, or canned pureed tomatoes

1 tbsp (15 ml) sugar

5 cups (1.2 L) chicken or pork broth (you can also use water)

Chicken stock powder, to taste (optional)

17½ oz (500 g) dried *mì Quảng* noodles

2 tbsp (30 ml) rice vinegar or fresh lime juice

1 trunk banana blossom

3½ oz (100 g) mint leaves, stems removed

3½ oz (100 g) perilla leaves, stems removed

1 large head leaf lettuce

10½ oz (300 g) bean sprouts

5 scallions, chopped

3½ oz (100 g) chopped cilantro

½ cup (72 g) crushed roasted peanuts

2 rice crackers broken into pieces

2 limes, cut into wedges, for serving

3 bird's eye chili peppers, thinly sliced on the bias, for serving

In Da Nang, it's a lot easier to find a place to eat this dish (*mì Quảng tôm thịt*) than pho. We natives can eat *mì Quảng* for breakfast, lunch, dinner, and anytime in between. It's the ultimate comfort food. There is no such thing as "the right way" to cook it. Every cook has his or her own variation and even the locals disagree with one another about the correct way to make it. The best bowl of *mì Quảng*, to Quảng people (from Quảng Nam Province/Da Nang City), has to be the one cooked by their mom. There are many versions of *mì Quảng*; you can enjoy it with chicken, eel, or snakehead fish. This recipe with pork and shrimp is the most traditional one.

INSTRUCTIONS

1. Add the pork, minced shallot, 1 teaspoon of the turmeric powder, ½ teaspoon each of the salt and black pepper, and 1 tablespoon (15 ml) of the fish sauce to a large bowl, and mix well. Season the shrimp with the remaining ½ teaspoon each salt and black pepper in a separate bowl and mix well. Set both bowls aside for 30 minutes.

2. Heat 1 tablespoon (15 ml) of the vegetable oil in a stockpot or a medium saucepan over medium heat. Add the minced garlic and cook and stir until fragrant.

3. Add the pureed tomatoes and 1 tablespoon (15 ml) of the fish sauce to the stockpot. Simmer over low heat for 5 minutes, until slightly thickened.

4. Meanwhile, in a separate large pan, heat 1 tablespoon (15 ml) of the vegetable oil over high heat and cook and stir the pork for about 5 minutes. Transfer it to a clean bowl.

5. Add 1 tablespoon (15 ml) of the vegetable oil to the same pan the pork was cooked in and cook and stir the shrimp over high heat for 1 minute. Add the sugar and cook and stir for another minute. Add the remaining 1 tablespoon (15 ml) fish sauce and simmer, uncovered, over low heat, until the sauce is almost evaporated, 8 to 10 minutes.

continued on page 140

6. When the tomato sauce thickens, add the chicken broth to the pot. Bring to a boil and add the sautéed pork belly. Adjust the broth to your taste. (I add 2 tablespoons, or 30 ml, fish sauce; 2 teaspoons chicken stock powder; and 1 teaspoon salt.) The broth should be saltier than a soup, but less salty than a sauce. Unlike pho noodle soup, we use a lot less broth for each bowl of *mì Quảng*.

7. Cook the noodles following package instructions. Add the remaining 1 tablespoon (15 ml) vegetable oil to the boiling water to prevent the noodles from sticking. If you want to dye the noodles yellow, add the remaining ¼ teaspoon turmeric powder 1 minute before the noodles are fully cooked.

8. To prepare the banana blossom, add the vinegar to a large bowl of cold water. Remove and discard the thick outer layers of the banana blossom and any flowers in between. Use a sharp knife (or mandolin) to slice it crosswise into paper-thin rings. Place the rings immediately into the water to prevent discoloring. Rinse the rings twice under cold running water and drain.

9. Cut the mint and perilla leaves and the lettuce into thin strips, about 1 inch (2.5 cm) thick. Mix with the banana blossom and bean sprouts.

10. To assemble the dish, fill the serving bowls half-full with fresh herbs and lettuce. Place a handful of noodles on top of the greens. Top with a few shrimp and pork belly slices, and ladle the broth over. Remember, the broth level should be lower than the noodles. Top with chopped scallion and cilantro, some crushed peanuts, and a piece of rice cracker.

11. Serve with the lime wedges, chili pepper slices, and a plate of the remaining fresh greens. Mix well with chopsticks before serving.

QUANG-STYLE NOODLE SALAD

SKILL LEVEL: Intermediate • **PREP TIME:** 20 minutes • **COOK TIME:** 15 minutes • **YIELD:** 4 servings

INGREDIENTS

Pork and Shrimp

7 oz (200 g) pork shoulder, pork belly, or pork loin, thinly sliced

2 tsp minced shallot, divided

1 tsp chicken stock powder, divided

1 tsp black pepper, divided

2 tsp fish sauce, divided

7 oz (200 g) shrimp, peeled and deveined

6 tbsp (90 ml) extra-virgin peanut oil, divided

1 tbsp (10 g) minced garlic

1 lb (454 g) bean sprouts

2¼ lb (1 kg) fresh or cooked *mì Quảng* noodles

7 oz (200 g) mint and/or Asian basil

2 tbsp (18 g) crushed roasted peanuts

Sauce

2 tbsp (20 g) minced garlic

2 bird's eye chili peppers

2 tbsp (30 ml) sugar

¼ cup (60 ml) fish sauce

Garnishes and Condiments

2 tbsp (18 g) crushed roasted peanuts

Few bird's eye chili pepper slices

Few drops sesame oil

> ## COOKING TIP
>
> If you cook dried noodles for this recipe, toss the cooked noodles with a couple tablespoons (30 ml) of vegetable oil to prevent them from sticking and to keep them slippery.

Extra-virgin peanut oil, locally called *dầu phụng*, is the ideal ingredient for this dish (*mì Quảng trộn*). However, even in Quang Nam and Da Nang, where *mì Quảng* originated, *dầu phụng* is not always available at the market. My mom special-orders it from a home factory that processes raw peanuts and extracts the oil themselves. Nothing beats 100 percent extra-virgin peanut oil for this dish. It has a higher smoke point than other vegetable oils and lends a wonderful nutty flavor to any food cooked in it.

INSTRUCTIONS

1. Place the pork in a medium bowl and season with 1 teaspoon of the shallot, ½ teaspoon of the chicken stock powder, ½ teaspoon of the black pepper, and 1 teaspoon of the fish sauce. Mix well and let sit for 15 minutes.

2. Place the shrimp in a different medium bowl and season with the remaining 1 teaspoon shallot, ½ teaspoon chicken stock, ½ teaspoon black pepper, and the 1 teaspoon fish sauce. Mix well and let sit for 15 minutes.

3. Heat 4 tablespoons (60 ml) of the extra-virgin peanut oil in a large wok or pan over medium heat. Add the garlic to the pan and cook and stir until fragrant. Toss the shrimp into the wok and sear both sides over high heat, 1 to 2 minutes. Transfer to a clean plate.

4. Add the remaining 2 tablespoons (30 ml) peanut oil to the wok. Add the pork and stir-fry over medium heat until it is no longer pink, about 5 minutes. Add the bean sprouts to the wok and stir-fry for 2 minutes, or until wilted. Return the cooked shrimp to the wok, toss, and turn off the heat.

5. **To make the sauce:** In a mortar and pestle, crush the garlic, chili peppers, and sugar into a fine paste. Combine with the fish sauce.

6. Add the noodles and fresh herbs to the wok. Drizzle some sauce over the noodles and adjust to taste with more sauce. Toss well. Add 2 tablespoons (18 g) crushed peanuts and toss again.

7. Transfer to a serving platter. Garnish with the crushed peanuts, chili pepper slices, and a few drops of sesame oil. Serve with the remaining sauce.

VEGAN QUANG-STYLE NOODLE

SKILL LEVEL: Intermediate • **PREP TIME:** 30 minutes • **COOK TIME:** 45 minutes • **YIELD:** 4 servings

INGREDIENTS

Vegetable Soup
6 cups (1.5 L) water
8½ oz (250 g) chayote or kohlrabi, peeled, with half cubed and half diced, divided
12½ oz (350 g) pumpkin, peeled and cubed
7 oz (200 g) taro, peeled and diced

Stir-Fry
1 leek or scallion, white and green parts separated and chopped
2½ tsp salt, divided, plus more to taste
3 tablespoons (45 ml) vegetable oil
14 oz (400 g) tofu, cut into 1-inch-thick (2.5 cm) steaks
¼ cup (60 ml) extra-virgin peanut oil or vegetable oil
2 index-finger-size pieces fresh turmeric, peeled and finely crushed
1 cup (100 g) mushrooms (such as straw and shiitake), cut into bite-size pieces
1 tsp mushroom seasoning powder, plus more to taste
2 to 3 tsp sugar, divided
4 oz (113 g) seitan (wheat gluten), cut into ⅛-inch-thick (3 mm) slices
½ tsp black pepper

Turmeric is the key to this dish (*mì Quảng chay*). **Fresh turmeric is best, but you can also use the powdered form. If using fresh turmeric, peel and cut it into small pieces, then put it into a plastic bag and crush with a pestle or meat tenderizer. Using a mortar and pestle is another option, but the yellow juice might splash and stain your clothes and hands. If using turmeric in powdered form, one teaspoon is enough for this recipe. Add it to the sautéed mushrooms and tofu along with the seasonings.**

INSTRUCTIONS

1. **To make the vegetable soup:** Add the water to a medium saucepan and bring to a boil. Add the cubed chayote and pumpkin and cook over high heat for 15 minutes, or until tender. Remove the chayote and pumpkin with a slotted spoon, transfer to a large bowl, and mash until smooth.

2. Add the diced chayote and taro to the broth in the saucepan. Cook for 7 minutes, then add 1 teaspoon of the salt. When the chayote and taro are tender, add back in the mashed pumpkin and chayote and remove the saucepan from the heat.

3. **To make the stir fry:** In a mortar and pestle, finely crush the white part of the leek with ½ teaspoon of the salt.

4. Heat the vegetable oil in a large pan over medium-high heat. Add the tofu steaks and fry until golden brown and crispy on both sides, about 3 minutes per side. Remove from the pan with a slotted spoon and transfer to a rack or a paper towel–lined plate to drain. Let cool, then slice into bite-size pieces.

5. Heat the peanut oil in a large wok or pan over medium heat until nice and hot. Add the crushed leek and fry until quite golden, about 1 minute. Add the crushed turmeric and cook and stir for about 10 seconds.

Noodle Bowl

1 head leaf lettuce, leaves torn into small pieces or shredded

3 sprigs each of herbs such as mint, perilla, and Asian basil, stems removed and chopped

2 lb (907 g) fresh or cooked *mì Quảng* noodles

½ cup (30 g) chopped cilantro

¼ cup (36 g) crushed roasted peanuts

2 limes, cut into wedges

3 cubes fermented bean curd (*chao*; you can buy 1-inch, or 2.5 cm, cubes in small jars at Asian food stores)

6. Add the mushrooms, 1 teaspoon mushroom seasoning powder, and 1 teaspoon of the sugar to the pan. Stir-fry for a minute over medium-high heat, then add the fried tofu and seitan. Mix well and season with the remaining 1 teaspoon salt and the black pepper. Mix in the green part of the leek to the pan and turn off the heat.

7. Add the stir-fry to the vegetable soup in step 2. Bring the soup to a boil and season to taste with salt and mushroom seasoning powder.

8. **To assemble the noodle bowls:** Fill the serving bowls half-full with lettuce and fresh herbs. Place a handful of noodles on top. Ladle the soup and veggies over the noodles. Top with chopped cilantro and crushed peanuts. Mix well and squeeze in a wedge of lime before serving.

9. In a small bowl, finely crush the fermented bean curd and mix with the remaining 1 to 2 teaspoons sugar (the consistency should be like cream cheese). Diners can add this extra to their bowl if desired.

PHNOM PENH NOODLE SOUP

SKILL LEVEL: Intermediate • **PREP TIME:** 45 minutes • **COOK TIME:** 1 hours 30 minutes • **YIELD:** 8 servings

INGREDIENTS

Broth

1 dried squid (hand size)
½ cup (90 g) dried shrimp
3⅓ lb (1.5 kg) pork bones
20 cups (5 qt, or 5 L) water
1 medium yellow onion, peeled
2 thumb-size pieces rock sugar
1 tbsp (15 ml) salt
6-inch (15 cm) piece daikon, peeled and cut into six 1-inch-thick (2.5 cm) rounds
1 lb (454 g) pork loin or pork shoulder

Toppings

1 lb (454 g) ground pork
½ tsp salt, plus more to season and to taste
Black pepper, to taste
3 tbsp (45 ml) plus 1 tsp vegetable oil, divided
3 tbsp (30 g) minced garlic
1½ tsp sugar, divided
2 or 3 shallots, minced
½ cup (75 g) Chinese salted preserved radish, minced (optional; you can buy this at an Asian food store)
7 oz (200 g) pork liver
Splash rice vinegar
12 prawns, peeled with tail on and deveined

This popular noodle dish (*hủ tiếu*) from Saigon is influenced by a Chinese-Cambodian dish called *kuy teav*. It is also known as Phnom Penh noodle soup. The toppings can be custom-made to order. You can choose to add shrimp, squid, liver, or pig intestines to your bowl. There are two ways to eat this dish: as a soup or as a dry version made with Black Sauce (see Cooking Tip, opposite) with the broth on the side.

INSTRUCTIONS

1. **To make the broth:** Tear the dried squid into small pieces. (You can heat it for 5 minutes in a toaster oven first to bring out the aroma). Soak the squid and shrimp in hot water for at least 15 minutes. Drain and rinse well.

2. Place the pork bones in a stockpot. Fill with enough water to cover them. Bring to a boil and cook for 5 to 10 minutes, until the impurities rise to the top. Drain the pot and rinse the bones well under running water to wash off the impurities.

3. Place the bones in a stockpot and fill with the water. (If you use the same pot as in step 2, make sure you clean it before putting the bones back. It is crucial for a clear broth.) Add the onion, rock sugar, salt, daikon rounds, pork loin, and shrimp. Bring to a boil and skim off the scum. Reduce the heat to low and simmer, uncovered, for 1 to 2 hours. Depending on the size, the pork loin will take 40 to 55 minutes to cook. Occasionally skim off the scum. If the broth reduces, add hot water to compensate, making sure you always have the same amount as when you started.

4. **To make the toppings:** Place the ground pork in a large bowl and season with the ½ teaspoon salt and black pepper. Add a splash of water and stir to separate the meat chunks.

5. Heat 3 tablespoons (45 ml) of the vegetable oil in a medium pan. Add the garlic to the pan and fry until golden brown. Transfer to a bowl and mix with ½ teaspoon of the sugar (this keeps the garlic crispy). Repeat this step with the shallot.

6. Stir-fry the minced preserved radish (if using) in the same pan as the garlic and shallot with the remaining 1 teaspoon vegetable oil. Season lightly with salt and the remaining ½ teaspoon sugar.

Noodle Bowl

21 oz (600 g) dried *hủ tiếu dai* noodles

1 bunch garlic chives (3½ oz, or 100 g), cut into 3-inch (7.5 cm) lengths or chopped

12 quail eggs, hard-boiled for 4 minutes

Fresh greens such as lettuce, Asian celery, and chrysanthemum

7 oz (200 g) bean sprouts

3 bird's eye chili peppers, thinly sliced on the bias

1 lime, cut into wedges

COOKING TIP

For the dry version, prepare Black Sauce: In a small saucepan, combine 3 tablespoons (54 g) oyster sauce, 3 tablespoons (45 ml) soy sauce, 1 tablespoon (15 ml) sugar, and 3 tablespoons (45 ml) water. Simmer over low heat for 2 minutes.

7. Place the pork liver in a separate medium saucepan and fill with enough water to cover it. Add the ½ teaspoon salt and vinegar. Bring to a boil and cook until done, about 15 minutes. Let cool and thinly slice.

8. When you pierce the pork loin with a chopstick and see no pink water coming out, it is cooked. Remove the meat from the stockpot and rinse under cold running water. Let cool, then thinly slice into bite-size pieces.

9. Place the seasoned ground pork in a mesh strainer and submerge into the stockpot until cooked. Use chopsticks to break up the lumps. Remove and transfer to a plate. Do the same with the fresh prawns.

10. **To assemble the noodle bowls:** Cook the noodles following the package instructions.

11. Fill the serving bowls with a handful of the cooked noodles. Top with ground pork, pork loin, pork liver, prawns, garlic chives, quail eggs, and fried garlic, fried shallot, and preserved radish. For the soup version, pour hot soup over the noodles and toppings. Serve Black Sauce (if using) alongside the dry noodle dish and a separate bowl of soup.

12. Serve with a platter of the fresh greens, bean sprouts, chili pepper slices, and lime wedges.

SANDWICHES

Bánh mì

VIETNAMESE BAGUETTE

SKILL LEVEL: Advanced • **PREP TIME:** 1 hour • **COOK TIME:** 30 minutes • **YIELD:** Three 8-inch (20 cm) baguettes

INGREDIENTS

1½ tsp active dry yeast

¾ cup (180 ml) lukewarm water (104 to 115°F, or 40 to 46°C)

1 tbsp (15 ml) sugar (optional)

2 cups plus 2 tsp (250 g) all-purpose flour (low protein and unbleached), divided

1 tsp salt

Bánh mì **is the most popular kind of bread in Vietnam. It can be served with beef stew (page 58) or stuffed with meat and vegetables to make the world-famous Vietnamese sandwich (page 153). I had never thought of making my own** *bánh mì* **until a number of viewers of my YouTube channel requested it. It was a long journey to come up with a recipe that works in a home kitchen. And I am so proud of myself that I did it!**

INSTRUCTIONS

1. In a large bowl, combine the yeast and lukewarm water. Add the sugar (if using) to help activate the yeast. Stir well to dissolve. Add 1 cup plus 1 teaspoon (125 g) of the flour and stir well to create a thick mixture with the consistency of pancake batter. Cover and let sit in a warm place for 2 to 3 hours, until bubbles appear all over the surface.

2. Add the remaining 1 cup plus 1 teaspoon (125 g) flour and the salt. Stir well with a wooden spoon until well combined. Transfer the mixture to a floured work surface and knead well until it forms into a smooth, soft, and elastic piece of dough. Kneading method: Fold the dough and use the wrist to push and stretch without tearing it. This helps the gluten to develop. You can alternate hands. Place the dough back in the bowl. Cover with a kitchen towel and let it rest in a warm place (95 to 98°F, or 35 to 37°C) for 1 hour, or until it doubles in size.

3. Carefully transfer the dough to the work surface, trying not to deflate the gas inside. With a scraper or a knife, divide the dough into 3 equal portions (each portion should weigh about 4½ ounces, or 130 g). Twist each portion inside out and form into a ball. Cover with a kitchen towel and let sit for 10 minutes.

4. Take out a portion, hold the side, and bang it 3 times on the counter. Use your wrist to roughly flatten it into an 8 x 4-inch (20 x 10 cm) rectangle. Roll it lengthwise and pinch the edges. Place both hands on top of the dough and roll it back and forth on the counter, applying more pressure with your fingers than your thumbs to shape it into a *bánh mì* form (broader in the middle and slimmer near the ends). Repeat with the remaining portions of dough.

continued on page 150

5. Place the shaped dough on a piece of parchment paper and cover with a kitchen towel. Let it rest for another hour, or until it doubles in size. In the meantime, preheat the oven to 450°F (230°C). Heat a baking sheet in the oven for at least 15 minutes before baking. Place a tray of hot water in the bottom of the oven.

6. To slash the baguettes, use a new box cutter or razor blade, held at a 45-degree angle, and make a quick and determined vertical slash down the center of the dough. Bake immediately after slashing. Remove the preheated baking sheet from the oven and lift up the parchment paper to transfer the shaped dough onto the sheet. Spray water on both sides of the oven and on the dough.

7. Bake for 20 to 25 minutes. After the first 8 minutes, spray more water on the baguettes and rotate the baking tray or the parchment paper to bake the baguettes evenly. If the bottom parts of the baguettes are not as golden as the upper parts, remove the water tray and lower the baking sheet.

8. Turn off the heat and let the baguettes sit in the oven for a few more minutes. The crust of the baguettes will continue to crack after being removed from the oven. You can actually hear the crusts cracking!

GRILLED PORK SANDWICH

SKILL LEVEL: Intermediate • **PREP TIME:** 30 minutes • **YIELD:** 6 servings

INGREDIENTS

6 Vietnamese Baguettes (page 149) or 2 French baguettes, cut into thirds

½ cup (118 g) Vietnamese Mayonnaise (see Traditional Vietnamese Sandwich on page 153)

10½ oz (300 g) pork liver pâté

1 lb (454 g) grilled pork (see Grilled Pork with Vermicelli Noodles and Fresh Greens on page 122)

6 small scallions, cut into 3-inch (7.5 cm) lengths

3 sprigs cilantro or mint

3 bird's eye chili peppers or jalapeño peppers, thinly sliced on the bias

1 cup (120 g) Pickled Carrots and Daikon (page 165)

Maggi Seasoning Sauce (you can buy this at an Asian food store)

This sandwich (*bánh mì thịt nướng*) is a popular variation of the Traditional Vietnamese Sandwich (page 153). Normally, *bánh mì* vendors grill the meat over charcoal next to their food carts. The smell of the pork grilling is the perfect marketing tool for their businesses. Who can resist that when driving past on an empty stomach?

INSTRUCTIONS

1. To assemble the sandwiches, slice the baguettes lengthwise and only halfway through so they open like a book. (If using a French baguette, remove some of the soft bread inside to make room for the fillings.)

2. Spread a thin layer of Vietnamese Mayonnaise and pâté all over the insides (you can microwave the pâté for 1 minute before using to make it soft and spreadable).

3. Stuff the baguette with the grilled pork, scallions, cilantro, chili pepper slices, and Pickled Carrots and Daikon to your preference, then sprinkle with a few drops of Maggi Seasoning Sauce.

TRADITIONAL VIETNAMESE SANDWICH

SKILL LEVEL: Intermediate • **PREP TIME:** 1 hour • **COOK TIME:** 1 hour • **YIELD:** 6 servings

INGREDIENTS

Red Pork Roll (*thịt đỏ*)

1.76 oz (50 g) roast red pork seasoning mix (such as Lobo brand)

½ cup (120 ml) water

1 lb (454 g) pork belly

Fish sauce or soy sauce, to taste (optional)

Sugar, to taste (optional)

Vietnamese Mayonnaise

2 egg yolks

¾ cup (200 ml) vegetable oil

Salt, to taste

Black pepper, to taste

Few drops fresh lime juice

Sandwiches

6 Vietnamese Baguettes (page 149) or 2 French baguettes, cut into thirds

10½ oz (300 g) pork liver pâté

10½ oz (300 g) Vietnamese ham (*chả lụa*), thinly sliced into half moons

1 small cucumber, thinly sliced into 3-inch (7.5 cm) lengths

6 small scallions, cut into 3-inch (7.5 cm) lengths

3 sprigs cilantro

2 bird's eye chili peppers or jalapeño peppers, thinly sliced on the bias

1 cup (120 g) Pickled Carrots and Daikon (page 165)

COOKING TIP

If you unwrap or untie the pork roll right after steaming, the pork will unroll and you won't be able to cut it into the traditional half-moon shape. Always refrigerate first.

Food carts selling *bánh mì* are on almost every street corner all over Vietnam. We're very creative with what we stuff inside the baguettes: you'll find everything from cold cuts to canned sardines, from roasted pork to transparent dumplings. This recipe shows you how to make every part of the most well-known Vietnamese sandwich: *bánh mì thịt*. It might be time-consuming to make, but the result is worth it.

INSTRUCTIONS

1. **To make the red pork roll:** In a large bowl, dissolve the roast red pork seasoning mix in the water. Add the pork belly to the bowl and coat. Let marinate in the refrigerator for at least 3 hours or overnight, turning occasionally to coat. The leftover marinade can be used to make red sauce. Simply bring to a boil and adjust to taste with the fish sauce and sugar. Reduce the heat to low and simmer for 2 to 3 minutes until slightly thickened.

2. Roll the pork into a log and wrap it tightly with plastic wrap. Use kitchen twine to tie it up. If you don't like to steam food in plastic wrap, simply tie the pork with kitchen twine. Steam for 45 minutes (or longer if you multiply this recipe). Let cool completely and keep in the refrigerator overnight. When ready to use, unwrap and cut meat into thin half-moon slices.

3. **To make Vietnamese mayonnaise:** Add the yolks to a medium bowl and whisk constantly. While doing this, gradually add the vegetable oil, a few drops at a time. Sprinkle with some salt and black pepper to enhance the flavor. As the mixture thickens, add a few drops of lime juice to loosen.

4. **To assemble the sandwiches:** Slice the baguettes lengthwise and only halfway through so they open like a book. (If using a French baguette, remove some of the soft bread inside to make room for the fillings.) Spread the Vietnamese mayonnaise and pâté all over the insides (you can microwave the pâté for 1 minute before using to make it soft and spreadable).

5. Stuff the baguettes with the Vietnamese ham, red pork slices, cucumber, scallion, cilantro, chili pepper slices, and Pickled Carrots and Daikon to your preference, then drizzle with red sauce.

MEATBALL SANDWICH

SKILL LEVEL: Intermediate • **PREP TIME:** 40 minutes • **COOK TIME:** 30 minutes • **YIELD:** 5 servings

INGREDIENTS

Meatballs

7 oz (200 g) jicama, peeled and shredded

2 cups (475 ml) water

1 lb (454 g) ground pork

1 egg

1 tbsp (15 ml) tapioca starch or cornstarch

½ tsp salt

½ tsp black pepper

½ tsp chicken stock powder

½ tsp sugar

Tomato Sauce

1 tbsp (15 ml) vegetable oil

1 tsp minced garlic

1 tsp minced shallot or white part of scallion

3 medium tomatoes, diced, or 1 can (14.5 oz, or 411 g) diced tomatoes, drained

1 tbsp (15 ml) sugar

1 tsp chicken stock powder

3 tbsp (45 ml) fish sauce

3 tbsp (48 g) ketchup

Sandwiches

5 Vietnamese Baguettes (page 149) or 2 French baguettes, cut into thirds

5 tsp Chili Jam (page 162)

6 small scallions, cut into 3-inch (7.5 cm) lengths

3 sprigs cilantro

2 bird's eye chili peppers or jalapeño peppers, thinly sliced on the bias

1 cup (120 g) Picked Carrots and Daikon (page 165)

You can either stuff a baguette with these meatballs (*xíu mại*) or you can plate them and spoon on tomato sauce. If you choose to do the latter, garnish with cilantro, thinly sliced onion, and crispy fried shallot, and offer the baguette on the side. Adding jicama to the meatball mixture helps keep the cooked meatballs juicy.

INSTRUCTIONS

1. **To make the meatballs:** Add the jicama and water to a small saucepan, and bring to a boil. Reduce the heat to medium and cook for 5 minutes. Drain, squeeze out the excess water, and chop finely.

2. In a large bowl, combine the ground pork, jicama, egg, and tapioca starch. Add the salt, black pepper, chicken stock powder, and sugar, and mix well. Let sit for 15 minutes.

3. Scoop out 1 tablespoon of the pork mixture and form it into a meatball. Repeat with the remaining pork. You will make about 15 meatballs. Steam the meatballs for about 15 minutes until they are no longer pink in the center.

4. **To make the tomato sauce:** Heat the vegetable oil in a large wok or saucepan over medium heat. Add the garlic and shallot, and cook and stir until fragrant. Add the diced tomatoes, sugar, chicken stock, fish sauce, and ketchup. Reduce the heat to low and simmer for 10 minutes. If you want more sauce, add ½ cup (120 ml) of water.

5. Remove the meatballs from the steamer, transfer to the saucepan, and combine with the tomato sauce. Simmer for 5 more minutes and turn off the heat.

6. **To assemble the sandwiches:** Slice the baguettes lengthwise and only halfway through so they open like a book. (If using a French baguette, remove some of the soft bread inside to make room for the fillings.) Spread some Chili Jam and drizzle some tomato sauce all over the insides.

7. Place 2 to 3 meatballs inside each baguette and use a spoon to break them into chunks. Add the scallion, cilantro, chili pepper slices, and Pickled Carrots and Daikon to your preference.

CONDIMENTS, PICKLES, AND SNACKS

Các món ăn kèm,
đồ chua, và ăn vặt

FRIED BREADSTICKS

SKILL LEVEL: Advanced • **PREP TIME:** 30 minutes • **COOK TIME:** 30 minutes • **YIELD:** 20 to 25 pairs of breadsticks

INGREDIENTS

2 tsp baking soda

1 tsp baking powder

1¼ cups (300 ml) water at room temperature, divided

4 cups plus 2 tbsp (500 g) all-purpose flour (10 to 11 percent protein)

1 tsp salt

1 tbsp (15 ml) sugar

Vegetable oil, for frying

COOKING TIP

If the protein percentage in your flour is lower than 10 percent, you might need to use less water. The amount of water should be somewhere between 1 and 1¼ cups (235 and 300 ml). If you want crispier breadsticks, use 1 teaspoon each of baking soda and baking ammonia to replace the baking soda and baking powder in this recipe.

This Chinese-influenced snack is popular in many Asian countries. In Thailand, it's called *pathongko*; in Indonesia, it's called *cakwe*; and in Vietnam, it has many names, including *bánh quẩy*, *quẩy nóng*, *dầu chéo quẩy*, and *dầu cháo quẩy*. Though it is normally served with soy milk or rice porridge, in northern Vietnam, it is common practice to dip the breadstick into pho broth. The heaviness of the fried bread is a nice contrast to the light, clear quality of the soup. Since the size of the pho bowl in Vietnam is rather small for hungry adults, eating *phở* with *quẩy* makes the meal more filling. This recipe is technically difficult, so it will take you a few tries (if not many) to get the perfect fried breadstick. Be patient and persistent!

INSTRUCTIONS

1. Place the baking soda and baking powder in separate small bowls. Add 3 tbsp (45 ml) of the water to each bowl (for a total of 6 tablespoons, or 90 ml). Stir well to dissolve.

2. Add the flour, salt, and sugar to a large bowl. Mix well. Make a well in the middle of the mixture and pour the liquids from the baking soda and baking powder bowls, along with the remaining water, into the well. Stir with a spatula until the flour absorbs all the liquid.

3. Knead the mixture with your hands for 1 to 2 minutes, until a rough dough forms. Cover and let rest for 20 minutes.

4. Remove and knead the dough for 1 to 2 more minutes. The surface will become smoother, but not completely smooth. Cover and let rest for another 20 minutes.

5. Repeat the process for a third and final time: Remove and knead the dough for 1 to 2 minutes. The surface should now be very smooth. Cover and let rest for another 20 minutes.

6. Remove and knead the dough for a few more strokes, then roll it flat to a thickness of ½ inch (13 mm). Cover with a slightly damp cloth and let it rest for 4 hours.

continued on page 160

7. Roll the dough flat to a thickness of ¼ inch (6 mm). Cut strips that are 1 inch (2.5 cm) wide, then cut these strips into bands that are 3 to 4 inches (7.5 to 10 cm) in length.

8. Dip a bamboo skewer in water and press it lengthwise into the middle of a dough strip. Repeat this step for half the strips, then stack the others on top to form pairs. Use the same skewer to again press lengthwise into the middle of the strips.

9. Place a large wok or pan over medium heat. Fill with vegetable oil to a depth of 2 inches (5 cm). Heat until the oil reaches 360°F (180°C), or test the temperature with a chopstick inserted into the oil: when bubbles appear around the chopstick, the oil is ready for deep-frying.

10. Quickly pick up one pair of dough strips, using both hands to hold near the ends. Stretch it out to double its length and carefully drop it into the hot oil. The dough will float to the surface in a second. Use chopsticks or tongs to keep flipping the dough until it puffs up into the shape of a traditional breadstick. Fry until golden brown. It's easier to manage if you fry one at a time. If the dough strips stick too tightly together, use chopsticks to loosen them so they have enough room to rise and puff up.

11. Remove from the wok and let rest on a rack or a paper towel–lined plate to drain the excess oil. These are crispiest when still warm. Serve within 4 hours of frying. Re-fry or heat in the oven for 5 minutes at 400°F (200°C) if you want to eat them the next day. You can also freeze fried breadsticks and re-fry or heat in the oven for 8 to 10 minutes at 400°F (200°C).

CENTRAL-STYLE PEANUT LIVER SAUCE

SKILL LEVEL: Easy • **PREP TIME:** 15 minutes • **COOK TIME:** 10 minutes • **YIELD:** 4 to 6 servings

INGREDIENTS

1 tbsp (15 ml) vegetable oil

1 tsp minced garlic

2 tbsp (32 g) peanut butter

3 tbsp (40 g) pork liver pâté

1 tbsp (15 ml) glutinous rice flour

5 tbsp (75 ml) water

1 cup (235 ml) chicken broth or plain water

2 tbsp (30 ml) Annatto Oil (page 170) or chili oil

1 tbsp (8 g) roasted sesame seeds

The original recipe for this sauce (*tương miền Trung*) takes triple the preparation time and calls for more than fifteen ingredients, including fresh liver, fermented soybean sauce, ground pork, and glutinous rice porridge. Here, I've simplified it for you. In central Vietnam, we serve this alongside Grilled Pork Vermicelli Noodle Salad (page 127), Grilled Pork Skewers (page 118), and Vietnamese Crêpes (page 37).

INSTRUCTIONS

1. Heat the vegetable oil in a medium pan over medium heat. Add the garlic and cook and stir until fragrant and quite golden.

2. Add the peanut butter and pâté to the pan, and cook and stir for 1 minute to break up the chunks.

3. In a small bowl, dissolve the glutinous rice flour in the water, then pour into the sauce in the pan to thicken.

4. Add the chicken broth to the pan and give it a good stir. Simmer over low heat for 3 minutes, until thickened, then remove from the heat.

5. Top with the Annatto Oil and roasted sesame seeds.

CHILI JAM

SKILL LEVEL: Moderate • **PREP TIME:** 20 minutes • **COOK TIME:** 40 minutes • **YIELD:** 8-ounce (227 g) jar

INGREDIENTS

10½ oz (300 g) red chili peppers or jalapeños, halved lengthwise
7 oz (200 g) tomatoes
1 head garlic, peeled
½ cup (120 ml) water
3 tbsps (45 ml) vegetable oil
4 shallots, thinly sliced
½ tsp salt
¼ cup (50 g) sugar

COOKING TIP

If you want to make the central Vietnamese–style sweet chili jam, increase the amount of sugar in this recipe to ½ cup (100 g) and mix in ¼ cup (32 g) of roasted sesame seeds.

You can use this jam (*tương ớt*) as a dipping sauce or spoon it on top of any dish. The chili jam served with pho is not as sweet as the chili jam served with other noodle dishes in central Vietnam.

INSTRUCTIONS

1. Bring a large saucepan of water to a boil. Add the chili peppers and tomatoes, reduce the heat to low, and cook for 2 to 3 minutes. Remove and transfer to a bowl of ice water to maintain the bright colors. Discard any seeds that might have fallen out in the process.

2. Peel the tomatoes, discard the seeds, and cut into small chunks. Put on gloves to remove the seeds of the chili peppers, then cut into smaller pieces. In a medium bowl, combine the tomatoes and peppers with the water. Blend in a blender until they break down into small chunks but are not yet pureed.

3. Finely crush the garlic in a mortar and pestle to form a paste.

4. Heat the vegetable oil in a large pan over medium heat. Add the garlic and shallots, and fry until golden brown.

5. Add the tomato–chili pepper blend, salt, and sugar to the pan. Stir well and simmer over low heat for 30 to 40 minutes, until the chili sauce thickens, occasionally stirring and scraping down the sides of the pan. Let cool completely before transferring to a sterilized jar with a lid.

6. Chili jam can be kept at room temperature for a week or in the refrigerator for a month. To keep mold from developing, pour a thin layer of vegetable oil on top before you seal the jar.

PICKLED GARLIC

SKILL LEVEL: Easy • **PREP TIME:** 15 minutes • **COOK TIME:** 15 minutes • **YIELD:** 16-ounce (454 g) jar

INGREDIENTS

4 cups (1 qt, or 1 L) water

2 tsp salt, divided

10 heads garlic (10½ oz, or 300 g, total), peeled and thinly sliced

2 cups (475 ml) rice vinegar

2 tsp sugar

6 bird's eye chili peppers, cut into 1-inch (2.5 cm) pieces

COOKING TIP

To prevent the garlic from turning slimy or light green after a few days, soak it in boiling-hot salted water. Also, thoroughly remove the sprouts at the core of the garlic cloves, as they can make the garlic turn green. Another important tip is to sterilize the jars and utensils. Make sure no oil is on anything you use, as that disturbs the pickling process.

In northern Vietnam, pho never comes with hoisin, bean sprouts, or fresh herbs; it is garnished simply with some chopped scallion and a sprinkle of black pepper. A few jars of additional condiments, such as fish sauce, chili jam, and pickled garlic, are often found on the tables at pho joints. Pickled garlic (_tỏi chua_) adds extra antibacterial properties to your pho bowl—after all, pho is considered medicine as well as food.

INSTRUCTIONS

1. In a medium saucepan, bring the water to a rolling boil. Add 1 teaspoon of the salt and stir to dissolve thoroughly.

2. Add the garlic slices to the saucepan and immediately remove the pan from the heat. Let sit for 5 minutes. Remove the garlic with a slotted spoon, shake off the excess water, and transfer to a large kitchen towel or paper towels. Evenly spread out the garlic and let sit for 2 hours, ideally in the sun, or in a dry, warm place or an oven with only the light on, to remove any excess moisture.

3. To make the brine, combine the vinegar, remaining 1 teaspoon salt, and sugar in a saucepan, and bring to a boil. Stir to dissolve, then turn off the heat. Let cool.

4. In a sterilized jar with a lid, combine the garlic and chili peppers, then pour in the brine to fully cover the garlic. Close the lid securely and store on the counter for up to 14 days. It is ready to serve after 3 days. It will keep in the refrigerator for a couple of months.

PICKLED CARROTS AND DAIKON

SKILL LEVEL: Easy • **PREP TIME:** 10 minutes • **YIELD:** 1½ cups (180 g)

INGREDIENTS

1 cup (110 g) shredded carrot
1 cup (110 g) shredded daikon
2 tsp salt
2 tbsp (30 ml) sugar
2 tbsp (30 ml) rice vinegar

COOKING TIP

Instead of shredding the carrot and daikon, you can cut them into thicker sticks. After peeling, cut them crosswise into 2½-inch-long (6 cm) segments, then cut them lengthwise into ¼-inch-thick (6 mm) slices. Stack the slices and use a wavy-edged knife to cut them again into ¼-inch-thick (6 mm) batons.

We Vietnamese love to have contrasting textures and flavors in our food. This pickle (*đồ chua*) is added to various dishes, from sandwiches to savory crêpes to vermicelli bowls. Its freshness balances out the greasiness of fried food. Its crunch, in concert with the sweet-and-sour taste, adds interest to any savory dish. If you don't like daikon, you can use kohlrabi or green papaya instead.

INSTRUCTIONS

1. In a medium bowl, toss the carrot and daikon with the salt. Let sit for 15 minutes. The salt will draw the moisture out of the vegetables, making them crunchier.

2. Rinse the carrot and daikon twice and squeeze out the excess water with your hands.

3. Add the sugar and vinegar to the bowl, and toss well. Let sit for at least 1 hour. The pickles can be stored in an airtight container for a few weeks in the refrigerator.

FISH SAUCE DRESSING

SKILL LEVEL: Easy • **PREP TIME:** 5 minutes • **YIELD:** ⅔ cup (160 ml)

INGREDIENTS

2 tbsp (30 ml) sugar
2 tbsp (30 ml) fish sauce
½ cup plus 2 tbsp (150 ml) water
1 tbsp (30 ml) fresh lime juice
1 tsp minced garlic
1 bird's eye chili pepper, minced

COOKING TIP

Not all fish sauce is equally salty, or has the same hints of sugar and lime. Adjust the recipe here to suit it to your taste. Having said that, of all the ratios I have tried, this one works best in most cases.

Most international cookbooks on Vietnamese cooking call this sauce *nước chấm*, but that's too generic; *nước chấm* simply means "sauce for dipping," and doesn't specify if the sauce is made with soy, mayonnaise, fish, or any other base. I call this *nước mắm pha nhạt* ("mild-flavored fish sauce") to be more specific and distinguish it from many other dipping sauces in Vietnamese cuisine (see photo, opposite).

INSTRUCTIONS

1. In a medium bowl, combine the sugar, fish sauce, and water, and stir well to dissolve. (The "magic" ratio to remember is 1:1:5, meaning 1 part sugar to 1 part fish sauce to 5 parts water).

2. Add the lime juice

3. Add the minced garlic and chili pepper last so that they stay afloat.

GINGER-FLAVORED DIPPING FISH SAUCE

SKILL LEVEL: Easy • **PREP TIME:** 5 minutes • **YIELD:** ⅔ cup (160 ml)

INGREDIENTS

1 thumb-size knob ginger, peeled
2 cloves garlic, peeled
2 bird's eye chili peppers, stems removed
3 tbsp (38 g) sugar, divided
6 tbsp (90 ml) fish sauce
6 tbsp (90 ml) water
2 tbsp (30 ml) fresh lime juice

This dipping sauce (*mắm gừng*) is great for serving with steamed squid, snails, beef, fried tilapia, and cooked duck. The ying factor in ginger is believed to balance out the yang factor in these proteins. It can also be used as a dressing for the Beef Shank Salad (page 35).

INSTRUCTIONS

1. In a mortar and pestle, crush the ginger, garlic, chili peppers, and 1½ tbsp (19 g) of the sugar into a fine paste.

2. In a small bowl, combine the fish sauce, water, lime juice, and the remaining 1½ tbsp (19 g) sugar and stir well to dissolve. Transfer the crushed ginger paste to the bowl to mingle with the sauce.

ANCHOVY DIPPING SAUCE

SKILL LEVEL: Easy • **PREP TIME:** 7 minutes • **COOK TIME:** 5 minutes • **YIELD:** 2 cups (475 ml)

INGREDIENTS

1 cup (165 g) chopped pineapple
1 cup (235 ml) water
4 to 8 tbsp (56 to 112 g) anchovy
   fish sauce, to taste
Sugar, to taste (optional)
Juice of ½ lime (optional)
1 tbsp (15 ml) vegetable oil
1 tsp minced garlic
1 tsp minced lemongrass
1 tsp minced bird's eye chili pepper

This very pungent sauce (*mắm nêm*) is used in central and southern Vietnam. Anchovy fish sauce is very salty, so I recommend diluting it with sugar and lime jiuce.

INSTRUCTIONS

1. Combine the pineapple and water in a blender. Blend well and transfer to a medium bowl.

2. Gradually add the anchovy fish sauce and adjust to your taste. The more sauce you add, the saltier the flavor. If needed, add some sugar and lime juice to taste (if using).

3. Heat the vegetable oil in a small pan over medium heat. Add the garlic, lemongrass, and chili pepper to the pan, and cook and stir until quite golden, about 30 seconds. Pour the hot oil over the sauce.

4. Mix the sauce well before serving.

VEGAN DIPPING SAUCE/DRESSING

SKILL LEVEL: Easy • **PREP TIME:** 20 minutes • **COOK TIME:** 5 minutes • **YIELD:** ½ cup (120 ml)

INGREDIENTS

3 to 5 dried shiitake mushrooms
½ cup (120 ml) hot water
⅓ tsp salt
1 tsp sugar
½ tsp mushroom seasoning
   powder
1 tbsp (15 ml) rice vinegar or fresh
   lime juice
1 tsp combined minced garlic and
   bird's eye chili peppers (optional)

Use this dipping sauce (*nước chấm chay*) as an accompaniment to vegan and vegetarian dishes (see photo, opposite).

INSTRUCTIONS

1. Soak the shiitake mushrooms in the hot water for 15 minutes. Remove the mushrooms for use in another dish. Extract the clear brown juice derived from the soaking (use a filter to remove the dregs) and combine with the salt, sugar, and mushroom seasoning powder.

2. Transfer the liquid to a small saucepan, bring to a boil, and stir to dissolve. Remove from the heat and let cool. Add the minced garlic and chili peppers if desired.

SCALLION OIL

SKILL LEVEL: Easy • **PREP TIME:** 5 minutes • **COOK TIME** 5 minutes • **YIELD:** ¼ cup (60 ml)

INGREDIENTS

3 tbsp (45 ml) vegetable oil (or pork fat)
½ cup (50 g) chopped scallion (green and white parts)
Pinch salt
Pinch sugar

COOKING TIP

You want the green color of a fresh scallion in this oil. After heating the oil to a high temperature, turn off the heat and add the scallion. The residual heat is enough to cook it, but not fade the color.

This oil, *mỡ hành*, **which translates to "fatty scallion," is made with pork fat. Diced fatback is heated until the liquid fat is rendered, and then scallion is added and cooked until wilted. I like to substitute vegetable oil for the pork fat to reduce the cholesterol. Just a hint of salt and sugar makes this oil even tastier.**

INSTRUCTIONS

1. Heat the vegetable oil in a small pan over medium-high heat until nice and hot.

2. Turn off the heat and add the scallion, salt, and sugar. Stir well until the scallion is wilted.

ANNATTO OIL

SKILL LEVEL: Easy • **PREP TIME:** 3 minutes • **COOK TIME** 10 minutes • **YIELD:** ½ cup (120 ml)

INGREDIENTS

½ cup (120 ml) vegetable oil
1 tbsp (15 ml) annatto seeds or paprika

SHOPPING TIP

You can buy dried annatto seeds in small packs in the spice section at most Asian food stores. If you are unable to located the seeds, use paprika as a substitute.

Annatto oil (*dầu điều*) is used to add color and richness to dishes (see photo, opposite).

INSTRUCTIONS

1. Heat the vegetable oil in a small pan over medium heat until it reaches 360°F (180°C), or test the temperature with a chopstick inserted into the oil: when bubbles appear around the chopstick, the oil is ready. Alternatively, you can use a microwave: Combine the annatto seeds and vegetable oil in a small bowl and heat for 1 minute on medium-high power.

2. Add the annatto seeds and turn off the heat. Let sit for 10 minutes. The seeds will turn the oil an orange-red color.

COFFEE DRINKS AND SWEETS

Đồ uống và tráng miệng

VIETNAMESE COFFEE

SKILL LEVEL: Easy • **PREP TIME:** 15 minutes • **YIELD:** 1 serving

INGREDIENTS

Special tool: Vietnamese coffee press

4 tsp sweetened condensed milk

4 tsp Vietnamese ground coffee (medium-coarse grind)

½ cup (120 ml) boiling hot water, divided

1 cup (140 g) crushed ice (optional)

Coffee fans cannot resist the bold taste of Vietnamese coffee (*cà phê sữa đá*) —so rich and creamy, it's almost like chocolate. Even non–coffee drinkers love it. You can skip the condensed milk to make black coffee served hot or with ice, but it's the sweetened condensed milk that makes this unique. Vietnamese coffee has to be made with a Vietnamese coffee press, which you can buy for just a few dollars at local markets in Vietnam or at Asian food stores.

INSTRUCTIONS

1. Place all parts of the coffee press in a bowl and pour hot water over them. Wipe dry with a kitchen towel. This is to make sure the coffee maker is perfectly clean so you get the best and purest taste out of the coffee.

2. Pour the sweetened condensed milk into a glass to form a thick layer at the bottom. Use a short glass for hot coffee and a tall glass for iced coffee.

3. Add the ground coffee to the base of the coffee press. Shake it gently to spread the coffee evenly. Screw or press the interior press tightly (but not too tightly) against the coffee grounds to tamp them down.

4. Place the coffee press on top of the glass. Add about 1 tablespoon (15 ml) of hot water and wait 30 seconds to let the coffee grounds absorb the water and expand. Fill the coffee press with the remaining hot water and cover with the lid.

5. The coffee will drip very slowly. After 6 to 7 minutes, it will stop. Set your coffee press on top of its overturned lid to prevent it from dripping onto the table. Stir well and pour into a glass of crushed ice for authentic Vietnamese iced coffee; if you like your coffee hot, place the glass in a bowl of warm water.

FRAPPUCCINO WITH COFFEE JELLY

SKILL LEVEL: Easy • **PREP TIME:** 20 minutes • **YIELD:** 2 servings

INGREDIENTS

Coffee Jelly
1½ tsp gelatin powder
¾ cup (180 ml) water
¼ cup (60 ml) Vietnamese Coffee
  (page 175), brewed
2 tbsp (30 ml) sugar

Frappuccino
½ cup (120 ml) Vietnamese Coffee
  (page 175), brewed
1 cup (235 ml) whole milk
3 tbsp (57 g) sweetened
  condensed milk
1 tsp vanilla extract
1 cup (140 g) ice
Whipped cream, for topping
  (optional)

COOKING TIP

When you make jelly with gelatin, the gelatin dissolves best in warm water. Bringing the water to a boil can make the gelatin fail. You can replace the gelatin powder with 1½ gelatin sheets. Soak them in cold water first before dropping them into the warm coffee mixture.

This coffee drink (*cà phê thạch đá xay*) **will give you a double dose of caffeine, with the Frappuccino and the coffee jelly!**

INSTRUCTIONS

1. **To make the coffee jelly:** In a small bowl, dissolve the gelatin in the water. Let sit for 5 minutes to bloom, then add the brewed coffee and the sugar.

2. Warm the mixture in the microwave for 1 minute on medium-high power. Alternatively, place the bowl in a larger bowl filled with boiling water. Stir to dissolve the sugar thoroughly.

3. Transfer the mixture to a 5-inch-square (12.5 cm) container and spread about 2 inches (5 cm) thick. Let cool, then chill in the refrigerator until set, at least 6 hours or overnight. When the gelatin sets, cut it into 2-inch (5 cm) cubes.

4. **To make the Frappuccino:** Add the coffee, whole milk, sweetened condensed milk, and vanilla extract to a blender. Top off with the ice and blend until smooth and icy.

5. Pour the Frappuccino into a tall glass. Add a few coffee jelly cubes per glass and top with whipped cream, if desired.

COFFEE MILK

SKILL LEVEL: Easy • **PREP TIME:** 10 minutes • **YIELD:** 1 serving

INGREDIENTS

3 tbsp (45 ml) sweetened condensed milk

1 cup crushed ice

¼ cup (60 ml) whole milk

¼ cup (60 ml) Vietnamese Coffee (page 175), brewed

Coffee milk (*bạc xỉu*) is a popular drink in southern Vietnam, especially for people like me who fancy drinking coffee but can't take that much caffeine. The name might sound strange even to my countrymen from the North, as it originates from a Cantonese word that means "a glass of milk with a little coffee." It has gradually become a staple offering on any coffee shop menu in central and southern Vietnam.

INSTRUCTIONS

1. In a tall glass, add the sweetened condensed milk to form a thick layer at the bottom.

2. Add the ice to the glass, followed by the whole milk.

3. Beat the brewed coffee with a frother until foamy, if desired. Top the glass with the coffee to reveal the layered drink. Stir well before serving.

THREE-COLOR DESSERT

SKILL LEVEL: Easy • **PREP TIME:** 15 minutes • **COOK TIME:** 1 hour 15 minutes • **YIELD:** 6 to 8 servings

INGREDIENTS

Green Layer
1 tbsp (15 ml) agar agar powder
4 cups (1 qt, or 1 L) water
¼ cup (50 g) sugar
⅔ tsp pandan extract (you can buy
    this at an Asian food store)

Red Layer
14 oz (400 g) dried kidney beans
    or azuki beans (or a mix of both),
    soaked in water overnight and
    drained
½ tsp baking powder
½ cup (100 g) sugar
Pinch salt

Yellow Layer
½ cup (100 g) peeled mung beans,
    rinsed, soaked in water for
    30 minutes, and drained
1½ cups (350 ml) water
¼ cup (50 g) sugar
Pinch salt

Serving
Crushed or shaved ice
½ cup (120 ml) coconut sauce
    (see recipe in introduction note;
    optional)

COOKING TIP

Parboiling the beans for
10 minutes helps remove their
toxins and tartness, and baking
powder helps speed up their
cooking time. Adding cold water
or a few ice cubes when cooking
helps the beans cook faster due
to temperature shock. Adjust the
amount of sugar to your taste.

This dessert (*chè 3 màu*) is a popular item at Vietnamese restaurants overseas. To make coconut sauce, combine 1 cup (235 ml) coconut milk with 2 tablespoons (30 ml) sugar and a pinch of salt. Bring to a boil. In a separate bowl, mix 1 teaspoon tapioca starch with 2 tablespoons (30 ml) water and add to the boiling sauce. Simmer on low for 1 minute, or until slightly thickened.

INSTRUCTIONS

1. **To make the green layer:** In a medium saucepan, dissolve the agar agar powder in the water. Let sit for 15 minutes to bloom. Bring the mixture to a boil while constantly stirring. When it boils, reduce the heat to low, add the sugar, and cook for a couple of minutes. Turn off the heat and add the pandan extract. Stir to blend the color completely. Transfer to a container and let set in the refrigerator or at room temperature for about 4 hours or longer.

2. **To make the red layer:** Place the soaked kidney beans in a large saucepan and fill with fresh cold water to cover them. Add the baking powder and bring to a boil. Boil for 10 minutes over medium-high heat. Drain and cover with a fresh change of cold water. Bring to a boil again, reduce the heat to low, and simmer until the beans are soft but not broken, about 45 minutes, adding cold water occasionally to compensate for the evaporated water. Add the sugar and salt to the pan. Simmer for another 10 to 15 minutes, until the sugar is well-absorbed.

3. **To make the yellow layer:** Place the mung beans in a small saucepan with the water and bring to a boil. Reduce the heat to low and cook until soft, about 15 minutes. When the beans turn mushy, add the sugar and use a blender or spoon to mash them until pureed. Keep cooking over low heat for 10 to 15 minutes and then transfer it to a container. When it cools down, it will thicken like a pudding.

4. When the green layer is completely set, loosen the edges and remove from the mold. Cut the jelly into thin strips.

5. **To assemble the dessert:** Add some crushed or shaved ice to a tall sundae glass. Layer a few tablespoons of the red bean layer, followed by the yellow layer of the mung bean pudding, and then the green jelly strips on top. Drizzle with some coconut sauce, if desired, and serve cold.

THREE-LAYER VIETNAMESE COFFEE MAGIC CAKE

SKILL LEVEL: Intermediate • **PREP TIME:** 30 minutes • **COOK TIME:** 50 minutes • **YIELD:** 8-inch-square (20 cm) cake pan

INGREDIENTS

3 medium eggs, whites and yolks separated
1 tbsp (15 ml) water
6 tbsp (75 g) granulated sugar, divided
6 tbsp (¾ stick, or 90 g) unsalted butter, melted
¾ cup plus 1 tbsp (90 g) cake flour
1 packet (0.6 oz, or 17 g) Vietnamese instant milk coffee powder
Pinch salt
1½ cups (350 ml) whole milk
1 tsp vanilla extract
Confectioners' sugar, for dusting (optional)
Coffee beans, for garnish (optional)

This cake (*"bánh thần kì" vị cà phê*) is magic! It is made with only one batter but forms three layers by itself during baking: one fudge, one custard, and one sponge cake. You might have seen it in other flavors like vanilla or chocolate, but I've given it a little twist with a Vietnamese coffee flavor, and it's great. You can dust the top with some powdered sugar or more instant coffee powder for a more polished look.

INSTRUCTIONS

1. Preheat the oven to 325°F (160°C). Line an 8-inch (20 cm) square cake pan with parchment paper.

2. Place the egg yolks in a large bowl. Add the water and 3 tablespoons (38 g) of the sugar, then beat with a handheld mixer until pale and creamy.

3. Add the butter a little at a time and mix well. Sift in the cake flour and instant milk coffee powder, followed by the salt. Mix well.

4. Gradually add the milk and mix well. Stir in the vanilla extract.

5. In a separate large bowl, add the egg whites and remaining 3 tablespoons (38 g) sugar, and beat with a handheld mixer until stiff peaks form. (Make sure the mixer whisks and bowl are clean before whipping.)

6. Gently fold the beaten egg whites into the batter with a whisk. Only fold 8 to 10 times; do not overmix. Pour the batter into the cake pan and even out the surface.

7. Bake for 45 to 50 minutes, or until a toothpick inserted into the center comes out clean. Let cool completely, then chill in the refrigerator for at least 4 hours or overnight for best results.

8. Before serving, dust with confectioners' sugar and garnish with some coffee beans, if desired.

COOKING TIP

It is crucial that you don't overmix the batter when folding in the egg whites. The bubbles in the beaten whites allow the top sponge-cake layer to form. The cake surface might look puffy in the oven, but it will wrinkle a bit when it cools. That's completely normal.

MIXED FRUIT DESSERT

SKILL LEVEL: Easy • **PREP TIME:** 20 minutes • **YIELD:** 8 servings

INGREDIENTS

1 dragon fruit, peeled and cubed

6 jackfruit segments, stone removed and cut into strips

1 ripe avocado, peeled, stone removed, and cubed

1 mango, peeled, stone removed, and cubed

½ pineapple, peeled, eyes and core removed, and cubed

16 longans or lychees, peeled and stones removed

2 cups (475 ml) whole milk

1 cup (235 ml) sweetened condensed milk

½ cup (120 ml) coconut milk

1 tbsp (15 ml) fresh lime juice

4 cups (880 g) shaved ice

½ cup (80 g) caramelized coconut ribbons (see Cooking Tip, below, for recipe; you can also buy these at an Asian food store)

½ cup (36 g) shredded young coconut flesh

We Vietnamese seldom eat dessert after a meal. Most Vietnamese desserts you might be familiar with are street snacks that we enjoy during breaks or between meals. We do love to finish our meals with fresh fruit—tropical fruit, of course—simply cut up and lightly flavored. This mixed fruit dessert (*sinh tố* or *hoa quả dầm*) is not for after a meal either; it's usually eaten late, during a night out with friends. Feel free to vary the fruit to what's in season or available in your area—maybe strawberry, kiwi, pear, or watermelon. For me, avocado and sweetened condensed milk are essentials. The rest can be customized to your liking.

INSTRUCTIONS

1. In a tall glass for each serving, add about 2 tablespoons of each fruit, ¼ cup (60 ml) of whole milk, 2 tablespoons (30 ml) of sweetened condensed milk, 1 tablespoon (15 ml) of coconut milk, and ½ teaspoon of lime juice.

2. Top with ½ cup (110 g) of shaved ice and garnish with a few caramelized coconut ribbons or shredded young coconut.

3. Use a long-handled teaspoon to slightly crush the fruit and mix well before serving.

COOKING TIP

You will slightly crush the fruit with a spoon when mixing and serving the dessert, so cut the fruit into small pieces. To make caramelized coconut ribbons, cut the flesh of a coconut into large pieces. Run a peeler along the cut side of the pieces to slice the coconut flesh into ribbons. Place the ribbons in a large pan with sugar (use ¼ cup, or 60 g, packed brown sugar for every 1 cup, or 80 g, coconut ribbons). Cook and stir constantly over low heat until toasted/browned, about 30 minutes.

INDEX

Note: Page references in *italics* indicate photographs.

ACKNOWLEDGMENTS

Of the over three hundred dishes that I have made and recorded videos for, a lot of these are recipes I never would have tried making if I hadn't had other people share them with me first. Like the Vietnamese baguette: why would you want to make that from scratch when you can buy one easily and cheaply? It's because so many of my international viewers longed to know the secret and requested a recipe. I can't thank my audience and supporters enough for their trust in my recipes and all the encouragement and love they often leave in the comments for each video.

A thousand thanks to Jeannine Dillon at Race Point Publishing for the proposal, encouragement, and guidance through the whole process of writing and publishing this book.

Many thanks to Evi Abeler for the professional food photos, Ha Tien Anh for the beautiful Vietnam location photography, Erin Canning for her tough editing and persistent questions, and Merideth Harte and Roger Walton for the magnificent design and layout of the book.

I would also like to thank Ms. Bay for excelling at her job as a caring nanny and also becoming my ingredient shopper and proactive kitchen helper while I was developing recipes for this book with a new baby. I made this book with my first child, Pho, always in my mind (and sometimes also literally in my arms). I can't wait for him to grow up and eat all the food I want cook for him.

I am fortunate enough to have a very understanding and supportive family: my mom and dad who always let me make the final decision, my sister, Summer, who has been my partner-in-crime for years, and my in-laws for taking care of my baby when I was rushed to meet the deadline for the final manuscript.

ABOUT THE AUTHOR

As the founder, producer, and host of the most popular Vietnamese cooking channel on YouTube, Helen's Recipes, Helen Le has helped her 350,000 international subscribers prepare delicious Vietnamese food in the easiest, fastest, and most authentic way. She is also a YouTube ambassador in Vietnam, a food writer for the website Danangcuisine.com, and the host of two cooking television shows that air in Asia: "Home-cooked Vietnam" on Asian Food Channel and "7 minutes for breakfast" on VTV7. She was on the short list for the Influence Asia social media awards in 2017. She lives in Da Nang, Vietnam. You can subscribe to her Vietnamese cooking YouTube channel at http://goo.gl/upfRRU.